IMPROV 101

Improvisational Exercises to Unleash Your Creative Spirit

Craig Zablocki

With Jill Zablocki

Published by Positively Humor

First printed in July, 2005

10 9 8 7 6 5 4 3 2 1

Printed in the United States of America

ISBN 0-9661834-1-X
Library of Congress Control Number: 2005905283

Published by
Positively Humor
634 Marion Street, Suite 102
Denver, CO 80218

www.positivelyhumor.com

Cover design by Debbie O.
Interior design by Jill Ronsley
jill@lemondropspress.com

For Charles

Acknowledgments

THANKS TO THE people who helped inspire this book. John Wagerbauer who asked me to try out for his highly successful improv troupe in Denver years ago at a time when it was a scary proposition. He taught me so much (and continues to) about improvisation. My friend Lisa Wilson and her mom Marleen who were great supporters to me. To my dad Charlie who helped a lot with the book, always said "geeve um," and had the nurses cracking up at the hospital right up until his death. To my cousin Scott who drew the illustrations. To my eight-year-old son Charles and his best friend Hanna who through the years have lived the principles of improv without even knowing it, making up games where they say yes … and … and showing me what's possible when we live in the moment with 100% commitment. To my brother Curtis and mom Carole who are a great support. And finally to the person who has been so awesome…the master of the keyboard, the big-kahuness, the left-brain to put it together … my sister-in-law Jill Zablocki who put everything together in a way that it could be easily read, understood, and used. She was awesome. Thank you.

TABLE OF CONTENTS

PREPENDIX: QUICK AND EASY 1

INTRODUCTION 3

CHAPTER 1: WHY USE IMPROV 101? 7
    Spontaneity and joy 7
    Think on your feet 9
    Live in the moment 9
    Commit 100% 10
    Personal growth 11
    Play 13
    Stop fearing judgment 14
    Change your perspective 15
    Synergy 16
    Acceptance 16
    Comfort with the unknown 17

CHAPTER 2: WHO CAN BENEFIT FROM IMPROV 101? 19
    Teachers and students 19
    Business professionals 20
    Families 20
    Care providers 20
    Anyone and everyone 21

CHAPTER 3: HOW TO USE IMPROV 101 23
    One-hour session guide 25
    Example one-hour session 26
    Showtime 27

CHAPTER 4: ROLES OF THE FACILITATOR 29
    Explain and clarify 29
    Provide feedback 30

Avoid evaluating content 30
Facilitate commitment 31
Facilitate safety and trust 32
Encourage participants to do vs be the best 32
Limit side talking 33
Solicit suggestions 33
Processing and discussion 35

CHAPTER 5: RULES OF IMPROV 39
Follow the directions 40
100% commitment 40
Acceptance 40
Denial (it isn't just a river in Egypt) 41
Don't try to be funny 42
Don't force it... 42
Don't think 42
Laugh with, not at 43
Turn up the volume 43
Show and don't tell 44
Avoid questions 44
Focus 44
Be specific vs. general 45

CHAPTER 6: GETTING STARTED 47
Warm-up activities 47
Getting their attention 48
Dividing the group and mixing it up 49
Lining up 51
Deciding who goes first 52
Pre-evaluation 52
Soliciting feedback 52

CHAPTER 7: WHOLE GROUP EXERCISES 55
Easy 55
Medium 64

CHAPTER 8: GETTING TO KNOW YOU 69
Easy 69
Medium 70
Hard 72

CHAPTER 9: PARTNERS EXERCISES 73
    Easy 73
    Medium 81
    Hard 97

CHAPTER 10: SMALL GROUP EXERCISES 111
    Easy 111
    Medium 130
    Hard 143

CHAPTER 11: GAMES SPECIFICS 151
    Basic flow of a game 152
    Advanced improvisation concepts 153
    Scene Development 155
    Endowments and influences 157
    Ending a scene 157
    Setting the stage 158
    Costumes 158
    Three-quarter stance 158

CHAPTER 12: IMPROV GAMES 159
    Easy 160
    Medium 169
    Hard 180

CHAPTER 13: CLOSURE ACTIVITIES 197

CHAPTER 14: A LIFETIME OF SPONTANEITY 203
    Commitment 203
    Acceptance 204
    No attachment to outcome 205
    Follow the rules 206
    No side talking 207
    Ways to improvise on your own 208

APPENDIX A: ONE-HOUR SESSION GUIDE 211
APPENDIX B: TOP FIVE RULES OF IMPROV 212
APPENDIX C: SOLICITING SUGGESTIONS 213
APPENDIX D: PROCESSING AND DISCUSSION 214
APPENDIX E: BENEFITS 215
ORDERING INFORMATION 225

QUICK AND EASY
(Bare Minimum)

THIS PREPENDIX IS for those of you who only have time to pick up this book and quickly prepare for an improv session with a group. If you are going to do the activities in this book more than once or if you have the time, you should fully understand the rest of the book, especially the chapters about the roles of the facilitator, the rules of improvisation and the games specifics. It will make your session(s) much more effective. In other words, 99.9% of readers should stop right now and jump ahead to the introduction. This section includes the absolute bare minimum for conducting an improv session. In it, I have tried to be as quick, succinct, brief, short, concise, and to the point as possible.

Step 1: Make a copy of Appendix A, the ONE HOUR SESSION GUIDE.

Step 2: Select the activities you want to do. Appendix E can help you choose; it lists the benefits to be gained from each activity along with difficulty levels. Write your selections and their page numbers on your copy of the ONE HOUR SESSION GUIDE. Get familiar with the activities you've selected.

Step 3: At the beginning of your session, read Appendix B, TOP FIVE RULES OF IMPROV, to the group.

Step 4: Go through your session as planned. For the partners exercise, the small group exercise and the game, you can read the description directly to the players. Bring up a volunteer for these to do a 5- to 15-second demonstration, and make sure everyone understands the rules of the activity before you start.

Step 5: Walk around the room during the activities, and make sure everyone is on task. Here's a quick list of some of your roles as a facilitator. They are discussed in greater detail in Chapter 4.

FACILITATOR ROLES QUICK LIST

☐ **Provide Feedback** about following the rules of improv and the activity. Be positive!

☐ **Avoid Evaluating Content** as funny or not funny, good or bad. Evaluate the *how* versus the *what*.

☐ **Facilitate Commitment** by encouraging participants to give it their all.

☐ **Facilitate Safety and Trust.** Players shouldn't feel they are being judged, ridiculed, or criticized.

☐ **Encourage Participants to Do Their Best, Versus Trying to Be the Best.** Avoid comparisons to others.

☐ **Limit Side Talking.** Put an immediate halt to any talking that isn't related to the session.

☐ **Solicit Suggestions** (see Appendix C).

☐ **Process and Discuss** (see Appendix D).

INTRODUCTION

SEVERAL YEARS AGO, I was invited to a comedy show unlike any I'd ever seen before. What I enjoyed most about it was that each scene in the show was totally new and was being created as it was being performed. It was as new for the performers as it was for me and the others in the audience. The question, "What's going to happen next?" was real for everyone in the room. This was very different from movies, where every aspect is controlled and the actors get numerous takes to get it right. It was unlike a play, in which every line has been rehearsed and every nuance of the performance is practiced over and over. Even most stand-up comics have perfected their memorized routine, but this was very different. It was true improvisation.

There is something riveting about not knowing what's going to happen next. It is exciting to be in the middle of something as it's being created, and it's engaging to know that what you're a part of is fresh and new. Each scene at this show was happening for the first time and regardless of the outcome (belly laughing whacky, or "Hmmm? What was that about?") it would never be seen again.

The actors that night demonstrated a heightened level of energy and resourcefulness while they performed scenes based on suggestions from the audience. Forced to work creatively together within the confines of a high-stress situation, they reminded me of the astronauts and ground crew for the Apollo 13 mission.

During its mission, the Apollo's main space capsule was damaged in an explosion. The crew had a limited amount of time to improvise a way to filter carbon dioxide from the air with only the items they had on board, or else.... Their creativity soared as they worked together as a team and communicated like never before. The improvised solution included suit hoses, cardboard, plastic bags and—yes, the key to many of life's problems—lots of duct tape.

3

Although each scene wasn't a life-or-death situation that night at the improv theater, the energy was phenomenal. We all wondered, "How will they ever pull off a Shakespearean play about their mom's favorite tuna casserole? Can they possibly create a poem about a car's rearview mirror? How can they make up a scene that goes forward and backward randomly?" It was almost magical the way it all came together for some of the scenes. Sure, one or two scenes flopped under the groans of a weak pun, but it was all intense, exhilarating, and even inspiring.

We were all terrific improvisers at one point in our lives. Children are excellent at making things up. As we grow older, our ability to pretend, to create, to improvise, diminishes. Many of us become conditioned by our various labels: father, student, smart, heavy, shy, special, weak, bad, strong, CEO, man, woman, old, pretty, caring, mean, stupid, introvert, American, Russian, sad, lonely, spastic, clever, clumsy, and on and on and on.... Every new experience isn't really new because of all the preconceived ideas we bring to it. How we view each other and situations is biased by our beliefs and conditioning. We think things like, this never works, he always does that, people from there are like that, men always..., women never..., applesauce is for sissies, and disco sucks!

Much of the time, we are acting out scripts that we have learned from our past and we don't even realize it. Think of all your reactions to situations. Are they really fresh and new, or are they just a reenactment of what you've always done before? If you say, "I'm shy" or "I'm not funny," is it true, or did someone convince you it is? Are we really improvising when we come to a new situation or are we bringing our conditioned past? Although we may think we're winging it in life, maybe we're not.

To totally embrace a life of improvisation, it's important to really see where we are going through life like a programmed robot reacting from patterns established from long ago. Improv can be an outstanding way to witness where we're stuck, where we have resistance, or where we're afraid. To really relate to each new experience in a fresh way—in a totally present and non-biased way—is what improv is about. If you understand this, then improv will be even more beneficial to you; it will allow you to try on another way of behaving.

I remember one time when I was the commencement speaker at a high school graduation; it was the most prepared I'd ever been. I spent

4

time writing notes, rehearsing, and really trying to make it good. The day of the ceremony, I gave my speech to a packed gym. Unlike when I improvise (and trust the moment), I was worried about doing what I'd planned to do. When we worry about doing the "right" thing, it's hard to be in the free mind-space where we can improvise. Anyway, the speech went okay, but several minutes later there was a glitch in the program. The tape to be played needed to be rewound, and the senior class president said they needed a few minutes. The superintendent looked at me and said, "Go say something." I thought, "Heck, I just gave my speech; what else do I have to say?" But I walked slowly to the podium, wondering what to do. I adjusted the microphone, looked out into the gym at all the parents, grandparents, and graduates staring back at me expecting something uplifting or enlightening, and I said, "B 12. Folks, that's 12 under the B." I paused. "O 65...65 under the O." No sooner did I finish than a proud father stood up in the middle of the bleachers and shouted, "BINGO!" He went along with it as we "verified his card" and confirmed that, yes indeed, he did have a bingo. He came forward and I awarded him the pen in my pocket as his prize. Several years later I ran into that superintendent. Neither he nor I remember anything about the actual graduation speech, but with a chuckle, he reminded me about the three minutes of "bingo" that saved the day.

A few years ago, while walking through the park with a friend, the topic of dancing came up. My friend said she hated to dance. When I asked why, she replied, "I just do." When I pressed her further, she didn't want to talk about it any more. I told her I thought she wasn't born hating to dance and perhaps it was related to something that happened during her childhood. She laughed off the idea, and we left it at that. Later that night, she called me up because she remembered tearing it up on the dance floor at a wedding when she was about four and realizing that people were laughing at her. She had made an unconscious decision to never put herself into a similar situation where people might laugh at her, and she wasn't even aware that this was still affecting her decades later. Improv can help everybody develop the confidence to overcome some of the fears that are limiting their lives. Getting comfortable being wacky and taking positive risks in a safe environment can help us overcome the fears that keep holding us back in the rest of our lives.

This book provides practical tools that groups of 2 to 2,000 and even individuals (Chapter 14) can use to tap into their creativity and spontaneity through improvisation exercises and games. Improv 101 can help people reclaim the enthusiasm, playfulness, creativity, honesty, and joy they had as children.

CHAPTER 1

WHY
Use IMPROV 101?

WHEN I USE improvisation exercises in speeches and workshops, participants often ask how they can learn to use these exercises. Although there are several books written on improvisation, the ones I have seen are written primarily for use by actors, so I wrote this book to help non-actors benefit from improvisation. I didn't create most of the exercises and games that are described in this book; people involved in the theater have used variations of many of them for years. But I believe the different ways of thinking and behaving that can be learned through these activities can benefit people in all walks of life, not just actors.

At one point in your life, you already knew most of what you can learn from this book. I'm talking about when you were about four years old. Young children are perfect in many ways. They are spontaneous and joyful, they live in the moment and commit to what they are doing, and they don't waste energy trying to avoid embarrassment or the judgment of others. Wouldn't you love to be like that again? If so, this is the book for you.

SPONTANEITY AND JOY

Learning to do improvisation can make you more comfortable with spontaneity. To me, this means thinking on your own and not letting yourself or other people put restrictions on your thoughts or actions. When we are free from both the good and bad opinions of others, we are free to be our true selves.

Spontaneity opens up a whole new world of possibilities, including an increase in the joy in your life. Joy comes from within; pleasure comes from external sources. A recent study found that the average child who is four years old smiles or laughs 400 times a day, while the average adult only smiles or laughs 14 times. In another study, on an assessment of creativity, four-year-olds scored nine times higher than high school seniors. The exercises and games in this book can give people a chance to reclaim some of the spontaneity and intrinsic joy they had as young children.

One afternoon, Michael was playing soccer with his fellow four-year-old teammates. It was a sight to behold. It didn't seem to matter who was playing offense, defense or goalie. They all swarmed around the ball, like moths around a porch light, and chased it around the field. Suddenly Michael stopped in the middle of the field while the rest of the swarm moved on. His parents were a little concerned. Was he physically hurt? Emotionally traumatized? They were relieved when, with a big smile on his face, he raised his arms into the air and exclaimed with shear joy, "I love this game!" He then rejoined the rest of the group. When was the last time you exclaimed "Man, I love shopping!" in the middle of a mall?

In that moment on the field, Michael didn't care what other people thought of him. He was excited and passionate, wasn't self-conscious, and was living in the moment. It wasn't about winning or losing; it was about having fun. When was the last time you did something only because it was just plain fun? Using this book will revive and nourish the ability of people over four years old to have some good old fashioned fun.

A few years ago, I was at a wedding reception sitting around with some people, doing what grown ups do in that kind of setting. You know, talking about something that has happened or something that is going to happen, but not doing any happening. Then I noticed three cute gals on the dance floor, so I decided to join them. They were sisters—three, five and eight years old. We took turns leading each other in fun, goofy dance moves. All of us crossed the threshold from inhibited to free, and we all had a blast. We made the jump. When you make the jump, magic happens and memories happen.

I think this jump was easiest for the three-year-old and most difficult for me, the conditioned adult in the group. It's something that becomes more difficult for us as we get older, probably because we build up a bunch of voices in our heads of people telling us what we should or shouldn't do, what's cool and what's not. Improv can teach you how to make the jump from inhibited to free. When you let yourself go in these activities, you can lose your self-consciousness. But just like you can't learn to ride a bike just by reading about it, you won't learn to lose yourself in spontaneity by *reading* this book. You will learn by *doing*.

THINK ON YOUR FEET

Part of what makes improvisation fun and exciting is that the same thing never happens twice, and nobody knows what will happen next. Because of this uncertainty, doing improv can really teach you to think on your feet, which is an important skill to have because life *is one big improvisation*. We make it up as we go along. Every conversation we have is improvised. Whenever we answer a question on the spot, we improvise the answer. There are no scripts for life. Learning to think on your feet in a safe environment will prepare you for challenges in the rest of your life.

LIVE IN THE MOMENT

When you do the improv activities in this book, it's almost impossible to be somewhere else emotionally or mentally. The uncertainty of improv generates energy and keeps people focused on what they are doing. The activities in this book can't be done mindlessly the way we sing a well-known song. They can't become trite.

How much of the time do you spend doing one thing and thinking about another? When you are with your kids are you thinking about work, and when you're at work are you worrying about your kids? If you spend your life thinking about what you did or what you need to do, you miss out on what you are doing. And that *is* life—what you are doing. It's a fact that when you are having a gut-busting belly laugh, it's impossible to think about or feel anything else. You can't be attached to your worries or your to-do list. When you really let yourself go with the activities in this book, it's a similar experience; there is no way you can *not* be present and in the moment. But you can only have this experience if you do these exercises with total commitment.

COMMIT 100%

Giving 100% in these activities (just like in life) is easier than giving 90% or even 50%. They can teach us to jump in with both feet. The jump I'm talking about is like the jump required to exit an airplane when parachuting. It's all or nothing, either you jump or you don't. There is no halfway.

In life, many things are easier when you are fully committed to them. One area where this is particularly true is in relationships. If you have a child, you know that many aspects of that relationship are easy because you are fully committed to your child. You don't look at other children and think about leaving your child for them. Your relationship isn't degraded because you are "still looking around." When your child wakes up in a bad mood or has a bad hair day, it doesn't cause you to consider leaving. Relationships with adults are the same way. If you are 100% committed, you don't waste time and energy thinking about leaving or about other options. You spend your energy making your relationship work.

Another area where 100% commitment is easier than anything less is with addictions or bad habits. For people who have a problem with drinking, it is easier to say, "I won't drink at all," rather than keeping the idea in the back of their minds that every now and then they will drink just a little bit. This leaves them needing to decide every day whether they are going to drink or not, or how much they will drink. The same is true for some people when it comes to eating healthy or exercising. Committing 100% and thinking of yourself as a person who doesn't eat candy or one who exercises five times a week gets rid of the need to make a decision about what you are going to do. The decision is already made.

The improv activities in this book can teach you to make a decision and commit to it fully. In improv, *what* decision you make isn't important; what's important is going *whole-heartedly* with the decisions you (and the other players) make. Doing improv is like being a fighter pilot. A fighter pilot has to make a snap-decision and then go with that decision. There's no time to vacillate between different choices, and after a decision is made, there's no going back. During a flight, a fighter pilot doesn't spend time and energy thinking about the choices he didn't make.

In today's world we are faced with an overwhelming number of choices for many of the decisions we make, from pasta sauce to vacation destination. You can spend a lot of time and energy making decisions and then be unhappy with them because you think about the benefits of the choices you didn't make. Sometimes it's best to quickly choose one of the acceptable options, commit to it and be satisfied with it. Doing these activities can help you learn this skill.

A few months after the Columbine tragedy, I put on a healing and humor program at Columbine High School. The message was to give the students and faculty permission to cry and to laugh again, to validate and allow any emotions they were feeling without repressing them. At one point in the program, we did some improvisation. A student, a teacher and I played the REPLAY game (page 178) in which we made up a scene about a plumber. We then replayed the same scene like a western movie, a Shakespearean play, and finally as an opera. Now, none of us were about to quit our day jobs because we couldn't carry a tune. But we performed our opera with 100% commitment and conviction, and because we did, the 2,200 students and faculty were riveted and laughed whole-heartedly. For three minutes, we were all totally present and engaged in the wackiness and joy of giving it our all. For those three minutes, we were all right there and had a break from our problems. These activities can help you learn to give it your all and really commit to whatever you do.

PERSONAL GROWTH

Doing improv can help you take yourself lightly so you can take more important things seriously. Slowly in the course of growing up, we learn to limit ourselves in ways that are not necessarily beneficial to our happiness and well being. Ask four-year-olds what they are going to be when they grow up and they tell you all sorts of things, believing every word of it. Ask most adults the same question and they'll probably say something like "I guess I'll be older." Young children take themselves lightly and believe they can do anything; adults often obsess about unimportant things, such as the opinions of strangers and whether their make-up is perfect. We can become stifled in our attempts to look good and to avoid looking bad. When we were young—before we experienced external constraints and influences such as rules, peer pressure, and the media—we could create without being attached to the creation.

Why is it that the number one fear for many people is speaking in front of a group, while death is rated seventh? What are we afraid of?

11

Being judged? Being ridiculed because we have a different opinion? Of looking bad? Once when I asked a woman in a group I worked with to come up in front of the group, she said with disdain, "I will not try anything; I will not be embarrassed." There she was (and here many of us are) living her life with *not being embarrassed* as her primary motivation. Do you know how much energy it takes to not be embarrassed? How many of us have traded in our dreams for the security of "not being embarrassed"? What if instead of devoting so much energy to not being embarrassed, we said, "It's okay to be embarrassed"?

I once met a man whose life-long dream was to be a teacher, but he went through a series of other jobs until he was thirty-five. When he honestly asked himself, "Why am I not living my dream?" he realized the answer went back to the seventh grade. He had given a speech in class, and all the kids laughed at him. After sitting down, he realized his fly was open. Naturally, he felt humiliated, so he made an unconscious decision never to get into a situation where something like that could happen again. He avoided his dream of being a teacher so he wouldn't have to speak in front of a group again.

This man lived safely, but did he really live? His primary motivation was *not* doing something rather than doing what he really wanted to do. For twenty-five years, he let that one experience control his life. Fortunately, he realized what was happening, went back to school and became an exceptional teacher who has had a positive effect on the lives of many kids. It saddens me that because of a single 60-second incident that he took so seriously, numerous kids missed out on the great teaching and leadership that he could have provided them.

How many of us make life decisions based on a two minute incident that happened in front of a few seventh graders who are no longer around? We walk around thinking, "Do I look okay? What does that person think of me? Don't trip. Is there something in my teeth?" And there is almost always something in your teeth. It's part of life. Instead of trying so hard to stay away from embarrassing situations, let's just get comfortable with being embarrassed. How about learning to see the humor in embarrassing situations?

Once while I was giving a speech, a piece of cracker flew out of my mouth and landed on the poufy hair of a lady in the front row. At that point, I had three choices: A) ignore it, B) nonchalantly flick it off her head, or C) ask for it back. I chose C. Learning to take ourselves lightly can free us to live life more fully and let go of some of the restraints we've put on ourselves.

The activities in this book can help make it okay to feel embarrassed. They will help you understand the importance of the question "In a hundred years, who's going to care?" Looking goofy in front of a group and surviving the experience can show us that it isn't the end of the world. If public speaking is the number one fear of adults and you can conquer that fear, then maybe the other fears will become easier to overcome.

PLAY

Watch a young child at play. She interacts with her environment without rules, and her natural creativity flows freely. I once watched a two-year-old as she was given a small container of yogurt. She cheered with joy, tossed the container into the air a few times, tried to balance it on her spoon, and pushed it around like a car before she proceeded to eat it. After she was finished eating it, what was left became finger paint on the table. What would an adult have done with the yogurt? Most of us would have thought of only one use. After our mothers told us time after time not to play with our food, we stopped considering all of the possibilities and began to just eat it or dislike it.

When was the last time you played just to play? Most adults play to win, sometimes at any cost. We put the emphasis on winning versus on playing. Children aren't attached to the outcome in the beginning, but they learn to be. When adults participate in a sport, we often do it to get better. We say things like "I'm going to go work on my free throws," or "I spent two hours refining my backhand." We don't just play for the enjoyment of it.

When kids play with Legos, they are just playing with Legos. They get totally into it, and there is no winner or loser. If you and I were to play Legos, it's likely that thoughts would go through our heads like "I should be doing something else," or "I'm not stopping until it's perfect," or maybe even "I'm going to save this forever." When I ask people "Do you like to play golf?" eight out of ten times they reply with something like, "I'm not very good." That wasn't my question. As adults, we often judge ourselves rather than just enjoying what we are doing, but as children we started out free from self-judgment.

Maybe our self-judgment keeps us from getting involved. For many adults, most of their involvement with sports (and much of life) is as a spectator. Kids live life "on the field"; most adults are "in the stands." Many of us heed the saying, "You won't miss any shots you don't take," so we end up living vicariously through the athlete on the field, the movie star on the screen, the child on the playground. The activities in this book can help bring back the playful spirit and creativity we all had as children and put us back on the field.

STOP FEARING JUDGMENT

Children start out free from the opinions of others. And then what happens? I recently got a glimpse into how the opinions of others affect us. I was in downtown Aspen at one of those great fountains where water randomly shoots up out of a bunch of different holes. I watched a three-year-old playing in the fountain. His shirt got wet, so he took it off. His shorts went next and were quickly followed by his underwear. He was free. He was totally happy. When he got a little chilled, he lay down on the hot cement to warm up. A couple of seven-year-olds came by, and one said to the other, "Look at that stupid kid." Luckily the younger boy didn't hear them and got to continue enjoying the bliss of the day, but I realized that if he had heard them he might have decided his behavior was wrong, and in turn, that *he* was wrong. It probably doesn't take very many experiences like this before we start to restrict our actions and even our thoughts.

In a talk to a group of 650 school superintendents, I started my speech with a request. "I need a volunteer to help me with an activity. It will be fun, you'll learn something new, and you'll be supported. Who would like to help me?" To my amazement, no one volunteered. With a great deal of curiosity, I stepped into the audience and asked, "Why do you think no one volunteered?" I waited for a response. Everyone in the audience was stone faced, the air thick with peer pressure.

Finally, I asked, "If I were to walk into a kindergarten class in your district and ask the same question, how many hands do you think would go up in the air?" The response from those who spoke up was, "All of them." I agreed and asked, "How about those in your fifth-grade classes?" The response from someone in the crowd was, "More than half." That's what I've experienced as well. Younger children are more likely to volunteer and love doing so. With older kids, self-conscious-ness has kicked in, and fewer put up their hands. By high school I'm lucky to get ten percent to volunteer and in a group of college stu-dents, it's around five percent. Wow, it seems like the younger we are, the more self-confidence we have. No wonder there aren't many self-help books for kids.

Now I'm not suggesting that superintendents should run naked through the fountains (especially on school grounds), but the activities in this book can help remove some of the limitations placed upon us by society and adulthood. A wise man called Dr Seuss once said, "An adult is just an obsolete child." I hope this book can help you to become less obsolete by helping you to regain some of the freedom from judgment and the creativity you had as a child.

CHANGE YOUR PERSPECTIVE

Several years ago, my son Charles and I were flying to Duluth, Minnesota when we hit some pretty rough turbulence. We were safely buckled in, but most of the adults on the plane reacted to the bouncing plane with gasps, gritted teeth, and white knuckles. Without thinking twice Charles, threw his arms in the air and shouted excitedly, "Weeeee!" I looked at the so-called "normal" responses of the adults and decided to join Charles. We both were having a blast riding the rollercoaster in the sky, when the lady across the isle, who looked terrified, scowled at us and asked, "What the hell are you doing?" Oh, the insanity of adulthood. Did she realize that none of us other than the pilots had any influence over whether or not the plane landed safely?

Does this kind of reaction—gritting our teeth, swearing and frothing at the mouth—help us to be more effective in our work and daily lives? Who had the better day? The stressed-out adults with high blood pressure, or Charles who went on a fun ride? Does plane turbulence cause stress? No, it's our reaction to plane turbulence that can cause stress. Or it can cause fun. You decide.

By practicing the techniques in this book, you will learn to see problems from a different perspective. We have a tendency as adults to get tunnel vision. These exercises can replace your single tunnel with a matrix of possible ways to look at the same issue.

Abraham Maslow said, "If the only tool you have is a hammer, you tend to see every problem as a nail." If you give a child that same hammer, he might dig with it, use it to pry something open, or dress it up and imagine it can talk and dance. Improv can teach you new uses for the hammer and help you to find some other tools.

There is a story about a young kid playing baseball alone in his yard. He'd toss the ball into the air and then swing at it with the bat. Time after time he would miss the ball. Another kid came along and told him he was a bad hitter. The first kid replied, "No, I'm not a bad hitter; I'm just a really good pitcher." It's all in the perspective.

SYNERGY

Improv is a very synergistic experience. Two or more people can do much more together than any one of them could do on his own. I once tried to drywall a ceiling in a room. I was determined to do it myself so I devised a big two-by-four "T" to help out. I had two ladders, the big "T" and my big ego to drywall the ceiling. It took seven hours. The next day I called a friend who came over to help. We did the other room (which was larger) in two and a half hours. That is synergy. You will see that when two or more people commit to the rules of a particular activity, synergy will happen. The magic of improv happens through collaboration. When I play the game ARMS EXPERT in my speeches, it is usually the best part of the speech. If I were trying to be entertaining by myself, or if the person doing the exercise with me was just standing there moving his arms, it wouldn't be very funny. But together it's a riot. We become much greater together than we would have been individually. This principle holds true in many other aspects of life, and these activities can help you understand that one plus one can equal five.

ACCEPTANCE

Stress is the difference between the reality of how things are and how we think they should be. Does a traffic jam cause stress? No, it's the desire to not be in the traffic jam that causes stress. In improv, as in life, you can't change what has already happened. If an improv scene heads in a direction you didn't expect (and they always do) it's imperative to go with the new direction rather than trying to head the scene back the way you thought it should go. After playing improv games for a while, you learn not to have expectations for a particular outcome. Then you can apply this learning to the rest of your life. In life, whenever you have expectations, you are setting yourself up for disappointment or resentment. Improv teaches us to say "yes" to life instead of "no." What we resist persists.

COMFORT WITH THE UNKNOWN

Let's face it. Nobody knows what's in store for the future. The very heart of improvisation is not knowing what is going to happen next. No two improvisations are ever the same, and improv only works when the people involved share the energy of what's happening right now instead of worrying about what's going to happen next. Learning this within the safety of the activities in this book can help you become more comfortable with uncertainty and the unknown in the rest of life. You can learn to look forward to it instead of dreading it.

No book can solve all of your problems, but if you do the activities in this book, you will learn some new tools (and relearn some old tools) that will help you live a more joyful and full life. In my 15 years of working with groups, I've seen people take positive risks and go through incredible transformations in a short period of time. I often receive comments like "Thanks, I didn't know I could do something like that; I've always been afraid to try." I saw these activities work an incredible transformation in a high-risk teen I worked with at a four-day workshop in Minnesota. On the first day, we played EVERYBODY GO... (on page 64). This kid obviously didn't want to be there, and when it was his turn to determine what the group said next, he grumbled, "This sucks." As the rules of the exercise require, the group repeated "Yeah ... this sucks!" with 100% enthusiasm. This wasn't the reaction he expected. The next day, he was a little more animated when he said "This sucks!"

At the end of the workshop, after about twelve hours of activities like the ones in this book, this same kid, Mister I'm-Way-Too-Cool-For-This, improvised a song about bugs (on the spot, in front of 300 people) and performed it in three different styles. The crowd was blown away by his performance because of his 100% commitment to what he was doing. He was transformed from taking himself very seriously to being able to use his creativity without fear or inhibitions. What he did that night, 99% of the people in the audience wouldn't have had the guts to do.

He wrote me a letter a few months later to tell me that his experience with improv gave him the confidence to make significant positive changes in his life. Try these activities and find out what they can do for you and the group you work with.

CHAPTER 2

WHO
Can Benefit From IMPROV 101?

VARIATIONS OF THESE activities have been around for a long time, but they've been used mostly in a theater setting. I have found tremendous application of these improv exercises by the groups and in the situations listed below.

TEACHERS AND STUDENTS

Both teachers and students can benefit from doing the activities in this book. Teachers will learn how to improve curriculum delivery, make learning fun, and keep students actively engaged. Teachers and students will learn to think on their feet and communicate more effectively. Students will become comfortable in front of groups and get an opportunity to experience being a leader as well as a follower. They'll get to know themselves and each other better, and they'll learn to respect each other's strengths. They'll get a chance to overcome inhibitions, take positive risks in a safe environment, and understand the benefits of cooperation.

These activities can be particularly effective with high-risk kids who tend to gravitate toward more creative ways of expressing themselves. This kind of learning experience has been effective in alternative schools where there are more students with the so-called attention deficit disorders. Because of their greater tendencies toward right-brain learning styles, these students learn well with these kinesthetic and experiential types of learning.

BUSINESS PROFESSIONALS

Do you get tired of boring meetings, predictable and dry presentations, or how about contrived and restricted discussions? The activities in this book can improve team building, communication, creative brainstorming, and problem solving. It's a fact that employees who are having fun and are better able to fully express themselves are more productive and stick with a company longer. With these activities, people will learn to think on their feet and become more comfortable in front of groups. The fact that most of these activities require two or more people can effectively demonstrate how teamwork leads to synergy. The workplace will become a more positive atmosphere leading to increased motivation, job loyalty, and productivity. People will feel freer to be themselves and make the mission of the organization important, not their ego.

FAMILIES

Throw out the TV (but before you do, watch *Whose Line is it Anyway?*), and start your own improv show. The activities in this book can make family time more fun and beneficial for everyone. Instead of turning on the newest reality show or playing video games, how about some in-the-moment experience? Use these activities in the waiting room, on the way to school, or while waiting for your food at Denny's. Play THAT'S A GREAT IDEA (page 126) to resolve conflict or make family decisions. The YES, AND ... NO, BUT ... exercise (page 92) is a great way to design a trip or build a consensus about a difficult situation. They're both fun ways to generate new ideas you might never have thought of. All of the activities are terrific for family reunions or get-togethers. They can be the gateway to more spontaneous, in-the-moment experiences with your family.

CARE PROVIDERS

Many of the activities in this book can be used in group homes, care homes, or anywhere that people are taking care of others. The activities can provide a creative outlet for energy and help put life back into the participants' daily routines. Some exercises can be used one-on-one with people who are having a particularly hard time.

Some years ago when I was a volunteer at a nursing home, Sam would walk slowly into my weekly group sessions. Inevitably, within the first five minutes he would be snoozing. I tried everything to get him engaged with the group. One day I went up to Sam and tried the MIRROR exercise (page 79). I said "Sam, look at me." He looked up and moved his face. I moved my face as he had. He stood up, so I stood up. I was mirroring his every move. The more energy he had, the more I had, and then his energy would increase even more. But the magic was just starting; soon we were singing and dancing "New York, New York" simultaneously. A worker came up and told me Sam hadn't been that alive in his 14 years at the nursing home.

ANYONE AND EVERYONE

Play the games at parties. Get some friends together to form an amateur improvisation group. Do the exercises in the car on long drives, around a camp fire, or while waiting in line to buy concert tickets. Invent your own games. Loosen up. Have fun. This is a great place to start.

CHAPTER 3

HOW
To Use IMPROV 101

I HAVE ORGANIZED this book to make it as easy as possible for group facilitators to use with both large and small groups. To conduct a one-hour session, all the facilitator needs to do is select one or more activities from each section as described in the ONE-HOUR SESSION GUIDE on page 25. Appendix A is a worksheet similar to this page that you can copy and fill in for different sessions.

The activities in this book all provide various benefits such as improving attention to detail, conflict resolution skills and non-verbal communication. Appendix E is a chart of the benefits provided by each activity. Use this chart to help you find activities to reinforce a specific idea or skill or if you want to pick a theme for your session.

Each of the activities is marked as EASY (E), MEDIUM (M) or HARD (H) both in the description and on the chart. If your group is new to these types of activities, start with easy exercises and games. As your group becomes more experienced and comfortable, move on to more difficult activities. Even with a highly experienced group, it is a good idea to throw in some easy and medium activities now and then.

Of course, any of the activities can be used alone if time is limited, if one exercise is particularly appropriate for an occasion, or if you are just playing for fun. If you have more or less than an hour available, you can alter the program. When working with a group, I recommend you use an introduction at the beginning (warm up activities and a whole group exercise) and a closing at the end to process what you've learned. It's like a sandwich; you can put as much or as little filling in the middle as you want. You can have a cheese sandwich if you have a short amount of time or a full-up Dagwood if you have a few hours.

For the partners exercise, the small group exercise and the game, you can read the description directly to the players or you can paraphrase it. For each of these, bring up a volunteer to do a 5- to 15-second demonstration, and make sure everyone understands the rules of the activity before you start. The facilitator leads the whole group exercises, so you shouldn't read those descriptions to the group. Make sure you are completely familiar with the whole group exercise you are going to use before you start working with the group.

When explaining the RULES OF IMPROV and the GAMES SPECIFICS, be very detailed if the group is inexperienced. With an experienced group, a quick reminder may be all that is necessary. However, you (as the facilitator) need to have a full understanding of the rules and your roles before you begin your session.

Immediately following the ONE-HOUR SESSION GUIDE is a sample agenda following the theme of teamwork.

ONE-HOUR SESSION GUIDE

☐ **Clarify the Top Five Rules of Improv** which are No Side Talking, Follow the Directions, Commit 100%, Accept, and Don't Try to Be Funny. You can read these to the group from Appendix B.

☐ **Do Warm-up Activities** for the body and the brain (page 48). I recommend at least one of these be used. This is when you set the tone for the session, so reinforce commitment and energy.

☐ **Do one of the Whole Group Exercises** to get things moving.

☐ **Process** as discussed on page 35. Keep it brief.

☐ **Divide the group into partners** (suggested techniques on page 50).

☐ **Do a quick "Get to Know You" exercise** (optional) from Chapter 8.

☐ **Do a Partner Exercise** from Chapter 9 .

☐ **Process** using the suggestions on page 35.

☐ **Divide into small groups** of 4 to 12 (suggested techniques on page 50).

☐ **Do a quick "Get to Know You" exercise** (optional) from Chapter 8.

☐ **Do a Small Group Exercise** from Chapter 10.

☐ **Process in small groups** using the suggestions on page 35.

☐ **Discuss the Games Specifics** in Chapter 11. Cover the basic flow of a game, miming, how to define *who*, *what*, and *where* and develop a scene, and three quarter stance.

☐ **Do a Game** from Chapter 12 in small groups, and/or bring three or four players to the front of the whole group to present a game.

☐ **Do a Closure Activity** from Chapter 13.

EXAMPLE ONE-HOUR SESSION - Teamwork

☐ **Clarify the Top 5 Rules of Improv:** No Side Talking, Follow the Directions, 100% Commitment, Accept, and Don't Try to Be Funny

☐ **Warm-up Activities:** Do physical stretches. Smile wide and hold it for 10 seconds, then frown as hard as you can for 10 seconds. Say "unique New York" five times fast.

☐ **Whole Group Exercise:** EVERYBODY GO... (page 64).

☐ **Processing Questions:** What did you notice about this exercise? How does it relate to teamwork? How many of you were embarrassed? Why? (Keep answers brief.)

☐ **Divide into Partners:** Everybody get up and find someone with the same length of hair.

☐ **Get to Know You Exercise:** In 30 seconds, tell your partner what you're proud of and what is a challenge for you.

☐ **Partner Exercise:** TWO SIDED (page 80).

☐ **Processing Questions:** What did you both have to do to make this work? How did you feel doing this exercise? How many of you had one idea while your partner had another?

☐ **Divide into Small Groups:** Merge your group of two with another group of two that has birthdays in months other than your birth months.

☐ **Small Group Exercise:** CIRCULAR MIRROR (page 121).

☐ **Processing Questions:** What did you experience while doing the exercise? What was difficult? How did it feel to be the leader? How did it feel to give up control? How does this relate to teamwork?

☐ **Game:** FORWARD/REVERSE (page 182).

☐ **Closure Activity:** HARMONIOUS HANDS (page 200).

SHOWTIME

If you have a long day or are working with a group over an extended period of time, you can plan a short show at the end of your session(s). Select four or five of the games that the players are familiar with and identify the volunteers who will perform them. If it is feasible, you can invite friends and family, perform for the other students at school, or you can go to a care facility or hospital and perform for the residents. The SHOWTIME GUIDE in the box below discusses the basics for conducting a show in front of an audience that is unfamiliar with the games.

SHOWTIME GUIDE

❏ Pick a time and place. Ideally the place will have theater-style seating, a stage area and good lighting. If you are going to have more than 100 people in the audience, you will need a sound system.

❏ Invite lots of people—friends, family, students, teachers, parents.

❏ Designate an MC before the show begins. The MC's responsibilities are to welcome the audience, explain improvisation, and discuss the conduct of the audience, including providing suggestions and keeping it clean.

❏ The MC solicits suggestions from the audience and then gives a brief explanation of the first game. For example: "In this scene about a carpet layer, the players will go forward as well as in reverse at the direction of an off-stage player."

❏ After about four to six minutes, the MC ends the scene and the audience applauds.

❏ Repeat four or five times with new games and suggestions

CHAPTER 4

ROLES
of the FACILITATOR

As THE GROUP facilitator, you have various responsibilities during the activities in this book. Each responsibility is described in detail below. Before you teach these activities to a group, it is a good idea to participate in them as one of the players. Do them with a few other people to help you fully understand the mechanics of each activity prior to your session. Through participating in them as a player you will also understand how it feels to do them.

EXPLAIN AND CLARIFY

Make sure the players understand how each exercise or game works so they are free to be creative within the structure of the activity. Most of the descriptions can be read directly to the players, or you can paraphrase them. In either case, a 5- to 15-second demonstration is always helpful. Encourage players to ask questions to clarify anything they don't understand. If players don't stay within the guidelines, there will be confusion in the group. When people are unsure of the exact parameters they will be tentative and hold back.

PROVIDE FEEDBACK

Another major role of the facilitator is providing feedback. Improv is risky, so it is important to focus on what is working well and to provide positive support and encouragement. The primary goal is for everyone involved to follow the rules of improv and the specific rules of each activity. This will allow players to experience a tremendous freedom that they cannot experience if someone is breaking the rules. They'll be free to express themselves and say things without fear of being judged or criticized. So when giving feedback concentrate on these three areas:

❒ Following the rules of improv in Chapter 5 ("Great job on commitment, Fillip." "Did you notice how Tom totally accepted Martha's offer to fly the plane?" "I really appreciate that nobody was talking other than the players.")

❒ Staying within the structure of the activity ("Everyone really did a great job of speaking only Gibberish." "Excellent job only using three words at a time.")

❒ Providing support to each other ("I saw how Anthony was really paying attention when it was George's turn to tell the story." "Nice job being loud enough so your partner could hear you.")

AVOID EVALUATING CONTENT

Although it may seem that the whole point of improvisation is to be funny, you should avoid praising a performance for being funny or clever. This is especially important during the games. Both good and bad judgments of how funny someone has been can inhibit the creativity of both the person being judged and of the other players involved. Everyone may feel pressure to be funny and start thinking too much, which will make them self-conscious. Like the words from a great halftime speech, "It's not whether you win or lose; its how you play the game." It is the process (the *how*) that is important rather than the outcome (the *what*). If you focus on the *how* of the activities, the *what* will take care of itself.

FACILITATE COMMITMENT

Often, the toughest role of the facilitator is to get the players to commit 100% to the activities. Tell the group, "The point is to give your best effort, not to be the best improv performer." If some players aren't 100% committed to the activities, no one will learn as much or have as much fun as is possible. Here's a math analogy: If three players are committing 80%, the net result of learning or fun is 240 fun units. If two players are giving 100% and one is only giving 95%, the net result is 295 fun units, but when all three players give 100%, the net fun result is 5,000 (or more) fun units. It's amazing how many of us will do something halfway and when asked how it was we say things like "I didn't get anything out of it," or "It was pretty stupid." How can we really know what we could have gotten out of it unless we gave it our full commitment?

If it seems that some people are not 100% committed, here's what I do to show them what 100% looks and feels like. I ask a volunteer to come up and have the group give her a standing ovation with all they've got (before she's done anything). Then I ask the group "How many of you just gave 100% in that standing ovation?" When people raise their hands, I have a few of them stand up and ask them to duplicate exactly what they just did. Then I pick the one who I perceived was holding back the most and ask him "Was that 100% for you?" Most of the time, he says "Yes." Then I ask "Could you double that for a $1,000?" He most likely says "Yes" again (with a little more enthusiasm). Next I ask, "If our lives depended on you giving five times more, could you do it?" Usually, he says something like, "Of course." It's then that the person usually laughs and gets it. What was 100% seconds ago is now more like 20%. Then I say something to the group like, "So you can see how we rarely give 100% to what we are doing, even when we think we are." Remember that the point is to get to the truth, *not* to make anyone feel wrong.

Some of the barriers to 100% commitment are self-consciousness, fear of failure, and worries about looking goofy or saying something stupid. You should look for participants who are giving it their all and use them as examples. Rewarding how they were *being* versus what they were *doing* may influence others to give more.

FACILITATE SAFETY AND TRUST

Ensure the environment is safe and the players trust each other. The best improv happens when people are willing to become vulnerable. When the environment is unsafe and people feel they are being judged, ridiculed, or criticized, they become self-conscious and worry about what they are going to say rather than just saying it. Without safety their spontaneity, learning, and fun will be limited. The STANDING O' (page 60) and ON THE SPOT CHEER (page 68) exercises (before an activity) are helpful in establishing trust and setting up a supportive environment within the group.

It's your role to make sure everyone involved understands that negative and sarcastic comments, cut downs, attacks against people, and making fun of each other are not allowed. Stop all activity when the first judgmental comment is made within the group (which is inevitable) to clarify for everyone what is okay and what isn't. It will pay off significantly in the long run.

The reason little kids are so free and spontaneous is that they feel safe from judgment. They aren't judged when they sing the ABCs in the car. Three-year-old Judy doesn't hear, "Mommy doesn't think you're hitting those high notes like you should." When playing with Lincoln Logs, Dad doesn't say, "You know Alex, Mike's four too, and his log cabins are so much more spectacular than yours." It is important that everyone involved in the activities feels safe to try new things without the possibility of being made fun of or being criticized.

ENCOURAGE PARTICIPANTS TO **DO** THEIR BEST, VERSUS TRYING TO **BE** THE BEST

Try to avoid comparisons. When people compare their performance to others they might think, "I can't be the best here." That's not the point. You want to encourage everyone to *do* their best, not *be* the best. If I told myself, "I'll never play golf like Tiger Woods," then I might never play golf at all.

LIMIT SIDE TALKING

Ideally, the only time participants are communicating with each other is within the context of the activity. Enforcement of this rule helps facilitate safety and trust. If you firmly establish this rule up front, you will have a smoother and more efficient session. To enforce this rule, clarify that side talking is any talking that isn't directly related to the activity. The first time a couple of people are talking to each other, stop what you are doing and point out that it isn't acceptable. If you don't enforce this rule the first time it is violated, it will be more difficult to enforce later. The time between activities should be silent unless it's in the context of the session. Whatever method you decide is the appropriate way of sharing after and between activities should be followed (raising a hand, discussing what you learned in partners, thumbs up versus thumbs down).

SOLICIT SUGGESTIONS

Some of the exercises and almost all of the games require a suggestion. The suggestion becomes a theme upon which the scene can take place. For some people, saying "Start a scene" without a suggested topic is like asking an English speaker who knows French to say something in French. Both situations can lead to brain lock. It is clear in the exercise description whenever a suggestion is needed for an exercise, and it should be assumed that all games start based on a suggested topic. Solicit suggestions from the audience or group using the requests or questions below, or feel free to make up your own questions. This list is also included as Appendix C for easy copying. Two or three suggestions can be combined to make things even more interesting. Go with the first response you hear and understand, as long as it's clean. You might want to explain to the audience (as well as the players) that you want to keep this at the G to PG rating. The task of soliciting suggestions can also be delegated to one of the players.

REQUESTS AND QUESTIONS FOR SOLICITING SUGGESTIONS:

❏ What is your favorite thing to do on the weekend?

❏ Tell me something you hate to do around the house.

❏ Name an outdoor activity.

❏ Give me a generic location.

❏ Name a place where you would never _____ .

❏ Give me two contrasting occupations.

❏ Name a country (or a state in the US).

❏ What is a goal someone wants to achieve?

❏ Give me a word beginning with the letter C (or any letter).

❏ Name two words that don't go together.

❏ Where's a place you love to go?

❏ What's something you'd find in a junk drawer?

❏ Tell me an achievement you're proud of.

❏ Give me a major in college.

❏ Tell me a place you would never hide.

❏ What is something you would love to do?

❏ Give me a three-letter word (or four- or five-letter).

❏ Make up a title of a story that hasn't been written.

❏ Tell me an occupation that is hazardous.

❏ Give me an emotion or state of mind.

Suggestions can be used in an unlimited number of ways. Often there is an obvious choice, but there are many more interesting ways in which a suggestion can influence a scene. For example: If the suggestion is baseball, the common reaction for beginners is to say, "Okay, let's go to the baseball game," and the scene consists of getting in the car, driving to the game, and watching the game. There are thousands of other ways the suggestion "baseball" can influence the scene. The scene could start with one player saying, "I got it, I got it, I got it" and making or missing the game-deciding catch. Players could also be stitching baseballs in a baseball factory or changing the numbers on the scoreboard in the outfield. Also, the suggestion does not have to be brought out in the beginning of the scene. With the baseball example, a grandma can be sitting in her rocking chair knitting when a baseball comes crashing through the window.

For beginners at improv, it's fine for the player who starts a scene to tell the other players the general who and where of a scene. If the suggestion is "pizza," the starting player might quickly say, "We're at chef school. You be the instructor and I'll be the student." Scene development is discussed in greater detail in CHAPTER 11: GAMES SPECIFICS.

PROCESSING AND DISCUSSION

After most exercises, I suggest you take a little time for processing and discussion. Processing and getting people to open up is an art more than it is a science, so take this information and apply it to your group with your own style. Ask questions that lead to discussion about what happened, how people felt, what was learned, and how it applies to everyday life or the theme you've picked (in that order). The questions should be open ended, like "What did you like about that exercise?" versus "Did you like that exercise?" It is also important to start with questions that focus on the positive aspects of the exercise and the strengths of the players. This can be accomplished by first having every group member say one positive comment, or asking the group something like "What went well?" Again, you should avoid talking about the content and focus on the process (following the rules of improv).

A list of questions that can be used for processing the activities is at the end of this section. This list is also included as Appendix D for easy copying. Start with one or two of the more basic level-one questions and continue on to the third or fourth level. You might not want to go to level four when you first start working with a group.

There are also discussion questions at the bottom of some of the exercises. Combine these with the questions in this section as you see fit. If you have a theme for your session, direct the questions toward that theme, or you can relate the activity to your group and what you do. There is space to write your discussion questions on the ONE-HOUR SESSION GUIDE at Appendix A.

Processing can be done with the whole group, or you can have participants discuss their answers to the questions in small groups or with partners. Some exercises just need one or two questions, and if time is limited, you can ask a question like "Give me a one-word description about how that exercise was," or "Tell me in three words what you learned from that." Of course, if you are just doing the activities for fun, you can do them without any processing.

As I said earlier, facilitating discussion after these activities is an art rather than a science. Your intention should be to get people to discover for themselves what they learned, so you shouldn't try to guess what they mean, prompt them too much, or answer for them.

> **Hint:** Use reflective listening to get people to go deeper with their responses. Rephrase back to them what they said and then wait for their response. For example: If you ask "How was that?" and someone replies with "Fun and hard," then you can say back "I hear you saying it was both fun and difficult." Then if you pause, they might say something else like "Yeah, that part where we had to follow the words is where I got stuck." Then you could say, "So you felt stuck," and so on. Essentially, you just rephrase what they said and then listen. Sometimes just pausing for a few seconds after someone replies will cause them to add more because they want to fill the silence. If someone says they couldn't focus on the activity, ask "What were you focused on instead?" and see where that leads.

Level-one questions (describe what happened)
- ❏ What are some observations about this exercise?
- ❏ What was easy (or difficult) about this exercise?
- ❏ What did you see or hear?
- ❏ What did you notice about yourself? About your partner?
- ❏ Use one word to describe what happened?

Level-two questions (share some feelings)
- ❏ How did you feel doing the exercise?
- ❏ Did you trust yourself?
- ❏ Did you trust the others in your group? Why? Why not?
- ❏ How did it feel to _____ ?
- ❏ What did others do that made you feel supported?

- ❏ What did you do to support others?
- ❏ Did you feel uncomfortable? Why? Is this familiar?

Level-three questions (make sense of what happened)
- ❏ What did you learn from this exercise?
- ❏ How does this exercise relate to _____ ? (teamwork, focus, work, etc.)
- ❏ What did you learn about communicating?
- ❏ When is it important to communicate with words?
- ❏ When are non-verbal forms of communication more important?
- ❏ What is trust and how do we learn to trust others?
- ❏ What was the point of this exercise?

Level-four questions (apply it to life)
- ❏ How does what you learned apply to your life?
- ❏ How is this exercise helpful for us?
- ❏ What piece of new learning can you apply to your life?
- ❏ What will you start, stop, or continue doing in your life?

CHAPTER 5

RULES
of Improv

IT IS VERY important that the facilitator set some guidelines for the group if these activities are to work optimally. The facilitator's task is to create safety and inspire people to commit to the activities by following the rules (guidelines) below. People generally want to be right and good, and when doing improv, they also feel like they should be funny. The best way to help players' natural talents and joy to shine through is *not* to reward scenes because they were funny, clever or witty; give positive feedback, rather, for the participants' commitment to their characters and for following the rules of improv.

The **TOP FIVE RULES OF IMPROV** are listed as Appendix B. They can be read directly to the participants, and they are all the players need to know to get started with a one-hour session of improv learning. However, it is important for the facilitator to fully understand all of the rules of improv so they can be discussed whenever there is a learning moment or when a specific rule is appropriate. If you are working with a group over an extended period of time, clarifying all of the rules up front can optimize the learning as well as the fun. A few of these rules apply primarily to the games, but you should have a full understanding of them even if you are only doing the exercises. Here is an in-depth discussion of the rules of improvisation.

FOLLOW THE DIRECTIONS

There are *specific* formats or rules for every activity that the players *must* follow. The facilitator should make sure everyone understands the directions and follows them completely. If they don't, there will be confusion in the group on the "hows" of the exercise or game, and they won't be able to fully let go within the boundaries of the activity. For example: In the game MANNEQUIN on page 189, one person moves everyone else's body. If a player who is not the mover moves his own body, he is breaking the rules and the scene won't work. When people are unsure of the exact parameters they will be tentative and hold back.

100% COMMITMENT

Committing 100% to the activities is the most important thing players can do to make them fun and meaningful. The idea of 100% commitment is a great concept that can be learned from improv. All people involved should give 100% to every activity or the activity will be difficult. A full 100% commitment is much easier than 70%, 80%, or even 90%. It's like jumping out of an airplane. You either do it or you don't. You can't be half-committed. If you are truly committed to the scene you are in, you should be *so* into your character that the character takes over. Things that would normally be distractions (like noise coming through a window, having a cold, a baby crying in the audience) will not bother you. People watching a scene become engrossed by it because the players are really into what they are doing, not because of witty lines or great acting. Define your character for yourself and really become that character. If you're a kid, really *be* a kid. If you're a cow, really *be* a cow. Strive to be 100% committed to the character and to the scene. When you are truly committed, you won't be thinking about what people are thinking of you or judging your own performance. Your full attention is on what you are doing rather than on thinking about what you are doing.

ACCEPTANCE

Acceptance in the context of improv means that everything that is said or done needs to be embraced as the true reality—without exception. When this is done, the scene is seamless and looks as though it was scripted and rehearsed. It seems real because everything is accepted as real, no matter how outrageous it becomes. Adults have a tendency to resist going to unknown places, and resistance will keep the magic from happening in these activities. One great thing about improv is that you can do the same exercise or game 1,000 times and it will never be the same. In other words, WE NEVER KNOW WHAT THE OUTCOME WILL BE! After some experience with these activities, you'll see how magical it is to give something 100% without knowing how it will end.

> **Hint:** Think "yes" instead of "no" to everything the other players say and do.

Here's an example of where a scene can go when the players accept rather than reject what happens: A boy brings his rocket ship to show his mother. When the mother spills Miracle Grow on the rocket, the boy says, "Let's get in." The mother says "Okay," and the rocket ship takes off. After running into a distant cousin in a far away galaxy and having lunch with him, with the help of OnStar, they make it home in time for dinner. When the father notices the hole in the ceiling, he says, "How many times have I asked you not to leave the galaxy on a school night?" If the mother had denied the spaceship growing, the scene might never have left the house.

DENIAL (IT ISN'T JUST A RIVER IN EGYPT)

The opposite of acceptance is denial. There are two main types of denials. One type happens when players don't accept what other players say and do. These denials often include someone saying the word "no." For example: One player says, "You must be the furnace repairman," and the other person replies, "No, I'm your mother." That really detracts from the reality of a scene. The only way to recover from a denial is to totally accept the denial as part of the reality. "Of course Mom, and you're great at fixing furnaces," would be a good response.

The second type of denial occurs when players aren't paying attention to what is happening. For example: One player clearly establishes a refrigerator (through miming) and the next person in the scene walks right through it. Both types of denial can happen when players are thinking about where they want the scene to go. Denials won't happen if players don't have preconceived notions about where the scene should go and if they totally pay attention to and accept what happens.

DON'T TRY TO BE FUNNY

Improv games are more fun to play and watch when players aren't trying to be funny. When players are trying to be funny, the scene becomes a contest to see who can be the wittiest, and it doesn't feel natural. Then the players don't react from the character's natural impulses. The atmosphere becomes one of competition and one-upmanship rather than being free flowing. When players aren't trying to be funny the *characters'* gut reactions combined with the restrictions of the game will be entertaining in and of themselves.

DON'T FORCE IT

Players should not "force" things to happen. A scene is being forced when someone tries really hard to direct it somewhere that feels out of place to the other players and to the audience. It leaves everyone asking "Where did that come from?" An improv scene can go anywhere (that's part of the beauty of improv), but it should get there in a "logical" or flowing way without any big leaps that make the audience or the other players feel disoriented. The urge to force things happens when the scene starts to break down, and the scene breaks down when players haven't established a definite *who, what,* and *where* (see page 154 for a full discussion). When the *who, what* and *where* are well established in a scene, the scene will take care of itself.

DON'T THINK

In improv, thinking gets in the way of learning and performing. When doing these activities, players need to understand the importance of *not thinking,* by which I mean not evaluating the ideas that come into their heads. It's impossible to commit 100% to an activity and to evaluate it in your head at the same time. Save the evaluation and processing until after the activity. Don't filter; just go with the first idea that pops into your mind.

Improv helps us get away from the constant evaluation of right or wrong, better or worse. After years of people telling us there is a right and wrong way to do things, we start to believe them. The facilitator should coach the participants not to think in terms of self-evaluation or criticism of their partner, the content, or anything else, until it is time to do so. This is a time to "just do it." The more you think about it, the more self-conscious you get and the less fun you will have. As the saying goes, if you have to eat a frog…don't think about it for too long.

LAUGH **WITH**, NOT **AT**

Laughing *with* other players is good; laughing *at* them is bad. The ability to take risks, be creative and have fun is possible only if players feel they are in a safe environment. That means that what they say or do might get laughed at (after all, having fun is the main point of these activities), but *who they are* or their *level of ability* won't be laughed at. Laughing *at* someone or making fun of them is completely unacceptable. There is one exception to this rule. It is okay to laugh at someone if that someone is you. No one is going to make up the perfect rhyme or the cleverest scene right away. That takes years of practice, and sometimes "mistakes" are more fun than something clever.

> **Hint:** Here is a good activity to further clarify laughing **with** versus **at**. Divide a chalkboard or large sheet of paper in two with a right and a left side. Ask players, "What makes you laugh?" Write down their responses in the left column without making any judgments. Then ask, "What are things other people find funny that are offensive to you?" Write down these responses in the right column. Inevitably, you will see similar items on both lists. This is a great way to start a discussion about offensive humor and the difference between laughing **with** versus laughing **at**.

TURN UP THE VOLUME

Not projecting voices is one of the most common problems that occurs during these activities, but it is also one of the easiest to fix. When people become nervous, they tend to speak softer and become more hesitant. Rather than letting this happen, nervous energy should be transformed into becoming larger, both in character and in volume.

Not understanding the other players will cause players to break character and ask "What did you say?" A good way to correct this is by taking a short line of dialogue and having a soft-spoken player say it several times, exaggerating the extremes until they reach a strong level of projection and finally get it. Try to clarify the difference between yelling and projecting.

SHOW AND DON'T TELL

Players should do things rather than talking about doing things. During the games, it is very important to perform actions and express emotions rather than telling the audience everything with words. For example: Instead of saying "Hi, I'm the happy elderly plumber here to fix your drain," the player should take on the characteristics of being elderly (slow, deliberate voice and walk, bent over a little) and act out fixing the drain while whistling a happy tune. He could then say something like, "I think I found the problem; it's a faulty washer." Likewise, it is better to feel annoyed, and let the character show that annoyance, than it is to say, "Boy, I'm annoyed with you."

AVOID QUESTIONS

In general, it is best not to ask questions in improv. One reason for this is because asking questions (like "What are you doing?") leads to telling instead of showing. Another reason is that questions don't contribute to the scene or move it forward. If one player begins a scene by miming digging a hole and then a second player asks, "What's going on here?" the audience might assume there is no relationship between the two characters (which there should be), and it tells them nothing about the *where* and *what* of the scene. A better choice would be if the second player entered the scene pushing a "wheelbarrow" and said something like "Dad wants the grave finished by noon." Asking questions forces the other players to carry the scene and prevents the synergy from happening.

FOCUS

The focus of the scene (the primary center of attention) should be on one or two players at a time and should switch naturally between players. Just like at an intimate dinner with friends, only one person at the table has the focus at any one time. It's most pleasant when the focus flows naturally among the dinner guests without anyone controlling the discussion or talking over the others. If one person tries to control a scene, the scene is ineffective, and it isn't much fun for the other players. Instead, there should be a constant *give and take* among the players.

A basketball team is a good analogy for sharing the focus. Only one player can have the ball at any one time, but the other players are contributing by looking for an opening or setting up a block. Nobody likes a ball hog, and a great basketball player doesn't always make the most points; she might contribute more by making assists.

Improv beginners often feel self-conscious or nervous. Sometimes, to compensate for their uneasiness, they feel the need to keep talking and they miss the offers that other players make. Only one person should talk at a time. If two or more players are competing for focus, they usually end up talking over one another and not listening to each other.

The facilitator should coach the players to contribute to the scene secondarily (through actions and expressions) whenever they aren't the main focus. For example: A player who doesn't have the focus at a restaurant can continue wiping tables without saying anything.

BE SPECIFIC VS. GENERAL

Some people are reluctant to add specific details to stories and scenes. With lots of specific dialogue and action, scenes are much more interesting and have more direction. Think about the difference between what the phrase "Let's go" adds to a scene versus, "Hurry! We've only go ten minutes to get to Grandma's potluck at the church." Everything becomes much more believable and vivid when there are lots of details, and it gives more direction to the scene. A person walking through the forest can simply walk across the stage the same way he'd walk across his living room. But a person who really sees the forest might carefully step around big rocks, duck to avoid branches and shiver from the cold. The exercise EMBELLISHMENT on page 84 is a good way to practice being specific.

CHAPTER 6

GETTING STARTED

THIS IS A collection of techniques I have found useful for working with groups. They can be useful anytime you are working with groups—not just when you are doing the activities in this book.

WARM-UP ACTIVITIES

Before doing any improvisational activities, it is a good idea to spend a couple of minutes warming up physically and mentally. Have the players do some of the following activities before each session.

Body:
1. Run in place and do jumping jacks. These exercises help get the blood flowing and physically prepare you for doing improvisation. Remember, this is just a warm-up, not a workout.
2. Stretch from head to toe. Make sure movements are slow and gentle, and hold positions for at least 15 seconds. Roll your neck and shoulders, touch your toes, and reach as high as you can.
3. Start by moving your fingers, and then add your wrists, then your elbows. Keep adding parts (arms, shoulders, upper torso, etc.) until you have your whole body moving.

Face:
1. Work your facial muscles by opening your mouth and eyes as wide as possible. Next, scrunch your face up by closing your eyes as tight as you can and pinching your mouth closed.

2. Stretch out your cheeks with your hands.

3. Smile wide and hold it for 10 seconds. Now frown as hard as you can for 10 seconds.

Vision:

1. Share a silent stare with someone in the room; no talking is allowed.

2. Look around the room and try to really notice the details of the objects and people. Count everything you see that is blue, or starts with the letter H, etc.

Voice:

1. Do tongue twisters slowly and then progressively go faster (toy boat, unique New York, lemon liniment).

2. Sing a familiar song quickly ("Row Row Row Your Boat", "Mary Had a Little Lamb").

3. Practice singing the scales—DO, RE, MI, and so on. Begin as low as you can and sing up to the highest note you can reach.

Emotions:

1. Repeat a familiar phrase in five or six contrasting emotions. Examples include happy followed by sad, excited followed by bored, or jealous followed by enamored.

2. Without speaking, try to feel various emotions while miming a simple activity such as typing or wiping a counter top. Begin the activity with no emotions and continue the activity with different emotions as the facilitator yells out new contrasting emotions.

Listening:

1. Sit quietly with your eyes closed and listen to your environment for approximately one minute. Discuss what sounds you heard and how the silence affected you.

2. Try to hear every word as the facilitator speaks softer and softer.

GETTING THEIR ATTENTION

It is sometimes a challenge to regain the attention of a group after a break or an opportunity for group members to interact with each other. Here are some effective ways to regain their attention.

1. Before breaking into smaller groups, tell them you will raise your hand when silence is needed and that when your hand is raised and group members see this, they should also raise their hands and be silent. The room will be quiet in no time. This works for adults as well as it does for kindergarteners.

2. Use a kazoo or other fun noisemaker to indicate that you want the group's attention. Avoid using whistles because they are just plain obnoxious.

3. Say, "If you can hear me, clap once." Some people will clap which should get the attention of others. Then say, "If you can hear me, clap twice." This will get the attention of even more. Then proceed with, "If you can hear me, clap three times." No matter how large the group, by the third clap, everyone will be paying attention. This can be modified in many ways by replacing "clap" with activities such as "stomp your foot", "jump up", "say hey", or "touch your toes."

4. Before breaking into groups, come up with an interactive jingle such as the facilitator saying, "dun dunda duda" and the group responding with "dun dun." Once group members become familiar with it, they will probably respond right away. Make up other response-inducing phrases that are appropriate to your group.

5. Speak very softly. People will pause to hear what you say.

6. Clap a simple rhythm and repeat it. Others will soon join you. Start with two claps, go on to three claps and then get crazy and more complex with it. You might clap twice, then look to the audience and clap twice with them (they usually pick up on this after a couple rounds). Next you might clap once, and snap your fingers twice, then look to them and repeat it with them.

DIVIDING THE GROUP AND MIXING IT UP

The following techniques can be used to divide a large group into smaller groups. Many of these techniques were actually used to divide the former Soviet Union into the various Fill-in-the-blank-istans. They can also be used to break up cliques, help group members get to know each other, and make sure no one feels left out. Each technique can be used alone or can be combined to form groups of any desired size.

Dividing Into Partners: Try one of these techniques to get people together who do not know each other very well. Have everyone quickly find another person they do not know very well who…

- ❏ has the same shoe size.
- ❏ is about the same height.
- ❏ has the same thumb length.
- ❏ has the same number of siblings.
- ❏ has a birthday in the same month.
- ❏ has a name that has the same first letter.
- ❏ doesn't like dividing-into-partners exercises.

These are just a few of the many different ways for pairing. Use your imagination to develop additional techniques.

Dividing Into Specific Group Sizes: Use the following techniques when you want to break a large group into smaller groups of a specific size.

1. Ask players to form a pair with one person they do not know very well using one of the Dividing Into Partners techniques. For groups of four, ask each pair to merge with one other pair. For groups of eight, ask them to merge again, and so on.
2. Tell the group that when you call out a number they must quickly divide into small groups of that number. When you call out another number, they must regroup with different people. The final number called out should be the desired group size. This can be a fun activity in and of itself. If time allows, have players do a quick activity to get to know each other (see Chapter 8) before each regrouping.

Dividing Into Specific Numbers of Groups: The following techniques can be used to divide a large group into a specific number of groups.

1. To divide a large group roughly in half, ask players with birthdays from January through June to move to one side of the room, and those with birthdays from July through December to move to the other side.

This can be varied to result in one to twelve groups. For example: Three-month intervals result in four groups and individual months produce twelve groups.

2. Ask everyone to close their eyes and decide if they are a horse, a cow, or a dog and indicate their choice by imitating the sounds these animals make. Then have them open their eyes, continue making the sounds, and form groups with those making similar animal sounds. Use any animals you can think of to form any number of groups.

3. Have everyone hold up one to four fingers (or any other number up to ten) behind their back. Have them show their numbers at the count of three and join up with people showing the same number. Palm up versus palm down can be used to form two groups.

4. Have everyone draw an imaginary circle in the air. Divide the group into those going clockwise and those going counter-clockwise.

5. Ask everyone to hop on one foot. Right footers go in one group and left footers form another.

6. Form groups according to favorite TV programs, family size, sock color, same eye color, or any other variation.

7. Make up your own.

LINING UP

Ask group members to line up according to one of the following criteria:

❏ from biggest to smallest shoe size

❏ in order by birthday

❏ in alphabetical order by *first* name (last name is over-used and the Zablockis are always at the end)

❏ in order of the last four digits of phone numbers

To add a challenge, ask the group to line up using one of the above techniques without speaking.

DECIDING WHO GOES FIRST

When deciding who should go first, use something like:

❏ the person with the shortest hair

❏ the longest last name

❏ the highest number of articles of clothing on

❏ the most money in their pocket

❏ almost anything can work

The lining up techniques can also be used to determine who goes first.

> There are an endless number of variations to these exercises and most other exercises in this book. Write variations you create in the spaces provided or in the margins, and email or mail them to us and we will put them in the next edition with an acknowledgement to you.

PRE-EVALUATION

This is a great way to make people aware of their commitment prior to an activity. Have them do a pre-activity evaluation by asking questions such as: "On a scale of one to five, one meaning 20% and five meaning 100%, how willing are you to participate today?", "How well will you support others today (or in this next activity)?", "How willing are you to take a risk today?", "How well will you listen this morning?" etc. This gets group members to ask not what the day can do for them, but what they can do for the day.

SOLICITING FEEDBACK

Try one of the following techniques for immediate feedback about how the group is feeling or understanding what is going on.

1. Ask the players to put up one to five fingers, with one finger representing, "I'm getting nothing out of this" and five fingers representing, "This is outstanding and incredibly beneficial." This technique can be used with various questions such as, "How comfortable are you?",

"How well do you understand the directions?", or "How did this exercise make you feel?"

2. Ask players to indicate their degree of understanding using their thumbs. Thumbs up means, "Yes, I understand," thumbs sideways means, "I sort of get it," and thumbs down means, "I'm totally confused." Other gestures can be used such as smiles, no expression, and ugly expressions; or standing, sitting and standing facing away.

3. Ask the players for a short description of how they feel or what they think of the exercise. The replies can be limited by specifying that they be one word, or two words, or by giving only ten seconds for each reply, etc.

CHAPTER 7

WHOLE GROUP EXERCISES

THIS CHAPTER INCLUDES exercises in which the leader directs a short activity while the entire group participates. These exercises will work with groups from 2 to 2,000. They are intended to get the group warmed up and thinking.

1	CLAP HAPPY

Easy

Directions: Have the players put their hands out in front of them about 12 inches apart as if they are about to clap. Tell them you will be saying "one, two, three, clap" and that they should clap (demonstrate) only when you say clap. Now say "one, two, three," physically clap your hands, pause for a second, and then say "clap." Some players will clap when you clap instead of when you say "clap." Keep doing it until the majority of the group gets it right. It might take several times.

| 2 | O.K. |

Easy

Directions: Say to the group, "I want to see how much you're paying attention today. Everybody make the O.K. sign with your right hand," and hold up the O.K. sign (thumb and index finger in a circle). Next tell them, "Place the O.K. sign on your chin," but as you say this, actually place the O.K. sign on your cheek. Keep the O.K. sign on your cheek and say, "We're not going on until everyone has the O.K. sign on their chin."

> **Hint:** This exercise is great for demonstrating that our actions speak louder than our words. At least 90% of the people will put the O.K. sign on their cheek.

Discussion: Ask ❏ How do kids (employees) learn from us. ❏ Are you a visual learner or an audio learner? ❏ Why was this exercise so difficult? ❏ Who was paying attention?

Gandhi was asked to by a mother in his village to tell her son to stop eating sugar. The diabetic boy needed to stop, and she knew he'd listen to Gandhi. Gandhi said to the mother, "I'll be back in two weeks." Two weeks later, he returned and told the boy "Stop eating sugar." The mother asked "Why didn't you just tell him two weeks ago?" Gandhi replied, "Two weeks ago, I was eating sugar."

3	ANOTHER O.K.

Easy

Directions: Make the O.K. sign with your hand (thumb and index finger in a circle) and place it a couple of inches in front of your forehead. Ask the players to make an O.K. sign and say, "What I need you to do is, without separating your finger and thumb, poke your head through the O.K. sign." Most people will look baffled or will try to push their heads through the O.K. sign. Eventually, someone will demonstrate the less obvious solution by taking the index finger of their other hand, putting it through the O.K. sign and poking their head with it.

4	WAY TO GO

Easy

Directions: In a circle and as a group, have players clap hands on thighs twice, clap hands together twice, snap fingers twice, and then with index fingers pointing to a person who has just accomplished something (like giving a speech or performing in front of the group) say, "Way to go, Lori." The phrase can be modified to fit the situation and group, and the loudness and number of movements can be varied.

> **Hint:** Each time you do it you can vary the claps and the movement. After a while, randomly pick people to make them up. They shouldn't have time to think; they should immediately improvise it.

5	MEGA MIRROR

Easy

Directions: Stand at the front of the group and tell them to mirror your actions. They should try to move simultaneously with you. Start slowly with simple arm and head movements and then add facial expressions and progressively wackier movements.

> **Hint:** Remember to use really slow movements at first. The participants must be focused on you and can't be doing any other activity at the same time.

Variations:
1. Rotate different group members into the role of leader.
2. Speak slowly while the group tries to speak your words simultaneously with you.

Discussion: This exercise works best when players take themselves lightly and focus on something outside themselves—the leader. Discuss how the group members should do the same thing with their dreams. They should take themselves lightly but focus seriously on the dream. If they do this, embarrassment and fears of failure or looking foolish will not get in the way.

It is the supreme art of the teacher to awaken joy in creative expression and knowledge.

Albert Einstein

6   CRISS, CROSS, CLAP

Easy

Directions: Stand sideways in front of the group with your arms extended out in front of your body at the two and four o'clock positions (see the illustration). Explain to the group that whenever your hands are horizontally lined up with one another, everyone should clap. Begin moving your arms in an up and down scissors-like movement. Start out by alternating arm positions slowly, resulting in single claps from the group. Then slowly speed up the arm movements to create sustained applause from the group.

Hint: Tease the group occasionally by stopping in mid-motion, before your hands cross. This will teach them not to anticipate.

To appreciate nonsense requires a serious interest in life.
Gelett Burgess

7	STANDING O'

Easy

Directions: When you bring someone forward to work in front of the group, give them a standing ovation *before* they do something. Say something like, "Okay, when I count to three, we're going to give Gloria the biggest standing ovation she's ever had." The rule for a standing ovation is that everyone has to give the person a 100% sincere standing ovation, and the person receiving the standing ovation should be as receptive as possible.

Immediately after the first standing ovation, ask the audience, "How many of you gave 100%?" Usually around half of the people raise their hands. Have a few of those who said they gave 100% (but you suspect they didn't) stand up and repeat what they just did. Then ask, "Was that 100% for you?" They often say "yes." Then ask, "Could you double your energy for $1,000?" Usually they say "yes." Ask, "So does that mean you were only giving 50%?" They usually say something like, "I guess so." Then ask, "If 100% means all you have to give, how much did you just give?" Usually they admit to somewhere around 20%. The point is to get to the truth, *not* to make them feel wrong. Then you can say something like "Let's all do it again but closer to 100% this time." There will be a drastic difference from the first time. After repeating it, most people understand a "real" standing ovation, what it means to give 100%, and that positive reinforcement is contagious.

> **Hint:** The reason many people don't give 100% to the Standing O' is because they feel they need a reason. Supply them with some reasons such as "because this person took the risk to come up here today," or "because they are a unique human being." Convey the point that we should not wait for people to accomplish a great feat before we recognize them. Showing appreciation for people and accepting them before they do anything makes them feel safe in front of the group. It is important to get in the habit of recognizing people in a positive way even if they have not accomplished anything great.

Variations:

1. Explain to the group that if someone feels they need a standing ovation, all they have to do is ask for one and the rest of the group should stop what they are doing and give them a quick standing ovation. This works best when everyone is participating.

2. Invent your own enthusiastic variations of the standing ovation. The group could say "Go Curtis, Go Curtis" accompanied with hand gestures, "woo-woo-woo," or "he ain't a fake, he's Jake," etc.

Discussion: Ask ❒ How did it feel to receive the Standing O'? ❒ Did you feel the energy triple the second time? ❒ How often do we hold back in other areas of our life? ❒ When do we commit 100% to what we are doing? ❒ What did you learn about recognition? ❒ What did you learn about giving 100%?

Discovery consists of seeing what everybody has seen and thinking what nobody has thought.
                                        Albert von Szent-Gyorgyi

8	VISIONARY

Easy

Directions: Ask the players to sit with eyes closed (or lie down if appropriate). Ask them to sit quietly and imagine doing an activity that you will describe to them. It is important to be very descriptive and speak in a calming voice. Ask them to imagine the settings you describe with vivid colors, smells, noises, and tastes. The scene you describe does not have to be related to improvisation. It could be about a walk in the forest or a successful public speech. Ask them to try to really feel, taste, smell, hear and see what you describe. It will help them to "see" the whole experience and help them to be more detail oriented when performing.

9	GROUP BEAT

Easy

Directions: Designate one side of the group as Team A and the other as Team B. Tell each team they should clap once when you point to them. Practice by pointing once to Team A, then to Team B. After the group is warmed up, develop a pattern. For example: A, A, A, B, or A, B, B, A. Mix it up. Speed it up. Have fun. This exercise is guaranteed to keep the group on their toes.

It still holds true that man is most uniquely human when he turns obstacles into opportunities.

Eric Hoffer

10   COLOR VISION

Easy

Directions: Have players close their eyes and ask them to think of the color blue (or any other color you chose). After about 10 seconds, ask them to open their eyes and quickly look around the room and only notice blue items. Ask "What did you see?" and let them name the items. Then ask "Who saw something new?" Most of the group members will raise their hands.

Discussion: This exercise illustrates that we see what we are looking for. Some things were there all along, but were not noticed until they were searched for. We often notice what we are looking for and miss out on what we do not expect. Ask ❐ Are you looking for the positive or the negative things in your life?

Through spontaneity we are re-formed into ourselves. It creates an explosion that for the moment frees us from handed-down frames of reference, memory choked with old facts and information and undigested theories and techniques of other people's findings.

Viola Spolin

11   EVERYBODY GO . . .

Medium

Directions: Tell the group that you will say "Everybody go _____," with the blank filled in with a sound, a movement, or a combination of the two. After this, they should say (with 100% conviction and acceptance), "Yeah!" and then make the sound and/or do the activity. For example: You say, "Everybody go la, la." The group says, "Yeah! La, la!" This continues for one or two minutes with varied sounds and movements. Start simple and get progressively more complex and goofy.

Hint: Ask the group to give 100% to this exercise and really duplicate your actions. Speed up this exercise to make it more fun. This is a great exercise for getting the energy going, for loosening up, and for becoming more spontaneous.

Variations:

1. After the group gets going say, "Everybody go..." and then randomly point to a member of the group. The player pointed to must explode with some spontaneous expression (sound and/or movement) that is then repeated by the group.

2. In a circle, each person is the leader for one sound and/or activity. The leader role goes around the circle in order until everyone has had a turn to say, "Everybody go _____" with the whole group responding with, "Yeah! ."

Discussion: Ask ❐ How many of you were embarrassed? Why? ❐ Is there a difference between silly and stupid?

> *In basketball—as in life—true joy comes from being fully present in each and every moment, not just when things are going your way. Of course, it's no accident that things are more likely to go your way when you stop worrying about whether you're going to win or lose and focus your full attention on what's happening **right this moment.***
>
> Phil Jackson

12	THUMB DANCE

Medium

Directions: Have the group divide into partners for thumb wrestling. Bring a player to the front of the room and illustrate the thumb wrestling position. Tell the group that their objective in this exercise is to maximize the amount of money they get. (You might want to clarify that this is imaginary money.) Say, "Every time you hold your partner's thumb down, you get a dollar. Only hold the thumb down for a fraction of a second and then quickly start over. You now have 20 seconds to maximize the amount of money you can make. Ready, go." After 20 seconds, ask "How many of you made absolutely no money?" It is likely that many of the hands will go up. Then ask "How many of you made one to five dollars? Who made six or more? Did anyone make ten or more?" If partners hold their hands up for the higher amounts, bring them to the front of the group and give them 20 seconds to demonstrate. The group will probably make sounds of understanding. The only way to maximize winnings is to cooperate rather than to compete. There are two primary options for cooperating: quickly alternating who wins so that each player wins half of the time or allowing one player to win all of the time and splitting the money.

Variation: If you are working with a very large group and not much room, it might work better to bring four or five pairs of similar sized people to the front of the group and have them arm wrestle rather than thumb wrestle. The same rules apply for gaining money. Make sure you include both male and female pairs.

Discussion: Ask ❏ What did the partners who made a lot of money do? ❏ Why are we so competitive? ❏ What did you learn about cooperation? ❏ How can you create a win win situation in other parts of your life?

13	THREE'S A CROWD

Medium

Directions: Have three volunteers come to the front of the room and then get three different topics from the group (see page 33 to learn how to get suggestions from the group). Assign each player one of the topics and instruct them all to speak to the group at the same time on their assigned topics. The speakers should really concentrate on what they are saying and speak at the same volume level as the other speakers. Instruct the audience to listen to and try to understand all three conversations at once.

> **Hint:** This exercise is useful whenever people are having a hard time listening to others or when everyone seems to be talking at the same time. It is difficult for the group to understand all three speeches at once.

Discussion: Ask ❏ How many of you were able to understand all three conversations in their entirety? There should not be any hands and they will get the message.

Never say a humorous thing to a man who does not possess humour. He will always use it in evidence against you.
                                        Sir Herbert Beerbohm Tree

14	ON THE SPOT CHEER

Medium

Directions: To keep everyone on their toes during your session, you can say, "Throughout our time together, we'll have lots of volunteers, and *before* the volunteers do anything, a random person will create a cheer for them. I will randomly point to someone, and that person will immediately make up a cheer that includes the volunteer's name and is coordinated with some kind of movement." Then give a really simple example. After each person creates a cheer, the whole group should repeat it together. If some people are reluctant or unenthusiastic about repeating the cheer (which is highly likely the first time) you can light-heartedly say "We'll keep doing this until we all do it with 100% enthusiasm. Let's go." To mix it up after a while, ask for a rhyming cheer, one that involves standing up, or any other specification you can think of. Be sure to modify the cheers so that any people with special needs are included.

> **Hint:** People will initially think they can't come up with cheers on the spot, however, once they can get out of their judgment mind and understand that ANYTHING and EVERYTHING works, the cheers become very fun indeed. Use this to involve someone who is just sitting there.

Among those whom I like or admire, I can find no common denominator, but among those whom I love, I can: all of them make me laugh.

W. H. Auden

CHAPTER 8

GETTING TO KNOW YOU

THIS CHAPTER CONTAINS exercises that will help members of your group get to know each other better. Some of them are geared toward people who are just meeting each other and some will help people who've known each other for years get to know something new about each other.

15	MAKE IT UP

Easy

Description: Players will tell others something about themselves in a specified format. Choose a topic such as biggest fear, favorite activity, most difficult subject in school and why, or the famous person you relate to the most. Then determine the format for delivering this information, such as a one- or two-word description, one sentence, or in 30 seconds. In a circle, start with more basic items and get progressively more complex.

16	PRIDE AND DREAM

Easy

Description: Each player will say one thing they are proud of about themselves and one dream they hope to accomplish in the future. They tell about both incidents in the past tense, as if both were already true. For example: "I once worked my way across New Zealand," and "I once finished a half marathon." The rest of the group tries to guess which event already happened and which one has not yet happened.

> Hint: This is a great exercise for getting to know something new about each other and a good way to find out what others' aspirations are.

Discussion: Talk about how acknowledging accomplishments and making goals public can lead to encouragement and goal fulfillment.

17	NAME GAME

Medium

Description: In a circle, the first player introduces himself by adding a positive word to his name. The word should begin with the first letter of his name, such as "Mighty Mary." The next person says "Mighty Mary" and immediately says her own name in a similar way, "Powerful Patricia." This format continues around the circle with players listing *all* of the names that have been said before their turn. The last person in the circle has the most challenging position because that person has to repeat all of the names.

> Hint: This is a great way for people to learn and remember each other's name through repetition and word association.

Variations:

1. Continue around the circle until everyone in the group has repeated all of the names.

2. Say names with a hand signal or body movement ("Travis" along with a peace sign).

3. Add favorite foods to names ("Owen Cheese Chunks").

4. Put a silly sound in front of names ("Schubi Latisha").

5. Put a trait that players like about themselves in front of names ("Energetic Raoul").

18	WEATHER REPORT

Medium

Description: Players describe how they feel in terms of a weather report. The group sits in a circle and each member takes a turn. For example: One player might say, "I feel partly cloudy with a warm front on the way." This provides a chance to express feelings in a creative way.

Variation: Players describe their home life, school, work, etc., in terms of a weather report.

19	PROUD TO SAY

Medium

Description: In a circle, players take turns completing the phrase, "I am proud that I _____."

Hint: Go around the circle a number of times to provide the group members with the chance to draw on many of their achievements.

20 NON-VERBAL ESSENCE

Hard

Description: In partners, players will convey their non-verbal essences to each other. The players have about a minute to convey the essence of themselves to their partners without using written or spoken words. Player A conveys his essence to his partner first. Then Player B tells Player A what she thinks his essence is. For example: A person hugging his partner might show that his essence is love and compassion. Then it is Player B's chance to express herself non-verbally. The essence of people is what makes them who they are, what drives them, or what they feel their service to the world is. It is not what their hobbies are or what makes them happy. The facilitator should explain what essence means and give them a couple of minutes to think about their essence before they begin.

> **Hint:** Don't let the players know they can't use written or spoken words until right before they begin to convey their essence. Just before they start say, "Oh, by the way, you can't talk or write."

Variations:

1. If conveying one's essence seems too difficult for a group, have the players tell each other one or two important things about themselves without using words.

2. Have the players explain their most embarrassing moment without any words.

CHAPTER 9

PARTNERS EXERCISES

THESE EXERCISES WORK best with two players, but many of them can be modified for use with small groups. Most only take a few minutes and they can be just what the doctor ordered to energize people, get their creative juices flowing and help them to connect.

21	PASS THE OBJECT

Easy

Description: Players will pass each other imaginary objects. Without speaking or making any noise, Player A mimes using a specific object, such as a telephone. He then passes the object to Player B who uses it and throws it away. Player B then mimes using a new object, such as a yo-yo, and passes it to Player A or on to the next player if the exercise is done in a small group. This exercise is excellent for practicing basic miming skills.

> **Hint:** Persuade the players to really "see" the object so their miming is not sloppy.

22   ENDOWMENTS PRACTICE

Easy

Description: A player will read a text with changing emotions or influences. One player reads from a text of some sort (a book, a play, a famous speech, the lines of a song, etc.). Every 10 to 30 seconds, the second player shouts out an emotion or some other type of influence (a movie style, famous character, particular characteristic). When each new endowment is shouted out, the reader takes on that emotion or influence and lets it affect the way he is saying what he is reading without changing the actual words. (See page 157 for a discussion on endowments and influences.)

Hint: This is a great exercise for learning to continue a story line with a different emotion rather than denying what has already happened because of the new emotion. This concept can be difficult for beginners to fully grasp.

23	TRUST WALK

Easy

Description: In partners, one player is blindfolded, and the other player leads the blindfolded person around, outside if possible. If blindfolds are not available, the players can simply close their eyes. The seeing person should lead her partner over obstacles safely just by talking to him. No touching is allowed.

Variations:
1. The seeing player stands behind the blindfolded player, puts his hands on her shoulders, and directs her with his hands without speaking.
2. The players hold hands and the seeing player leads the blindfolded player around without speaking.
3. Create a game with a roomful of "cars." The blindfolded person is in front with the "driver" behind them, hands on their shoulders steering them around the room with the others. The drivers should be careful not to crash into any of the other cars.

Discussion: Ask ❒ What did it feel like to be led around? ❒ What did you have to do to trust the person who led you? ❒ How did it feel to be the leader?

Spontaneity is the moment of personal freedom when we are faced with reality, and see it, explore it and act accordingly. In this reality the bits and pieces of ourselves function as an organic whole. It is the time of discovery, of experiencing, of creative expression.

Viola Spolin

24	GROUND CONTROL

Easy

Description: A seeing player will guide a blindfolded player through an obstacle course. Mark off a rectangular area (approximately 5 by 10 feet) with chairs or tape, and set up an obstacle course of people, chairs, or other props in this area. Two players stand at opposite ends of the area; one of them is blindfolded. The sighted player can only use his voice to guide the blindfolded player through the obstacle course without the blindfolded player touching any of the props. If she touches a prop, she must go back to the beginning and start again. After the first player has made it successfully through the obstacle course, rearrange the props, and swap the roles of the two players.

Variations:
1. The blindfolded person cannot speak.
2. Players can only use sounds, such as claps increasing in tempo or a buzzing noise that increases in pitch when the blindfolded player gets close to an obstacle.

Discussion: Ask ❑ What did you learn about how important it is to listen? ❑ What style of communication worked the best? ❑ What was frustrating/easy for the guide? ❑ How is this exercise like communication at work? Home? etc.?

---

25   I LOVE YOU SO MUCH, BABY

Easy

Description: In pairs, the first player's objective is to get her partner to laugh by saying, "I love you so much, baby, but I just can't make you laugh!" She can repeat this phrase as outrageously as necessary to make her partner laugh. The objective of the second player is not to laugh. Funny actions can be used, but no touching or tickling is allowed. After the first player gets her partner to laugh, the players switch roles. The first player can play with her voice, be obnoxious, or sing the phrase in a strange voice.

> **Hint:** This is a great exercise to get people to be outrageous while trying to get the other person to laugh. For the other person, it's a great exercise to "stay in character" or keep a straight face under pressure.

Variation: The phrase is changed to, "I love you so much, baby, but I just can't make you smile," and the first player tries to make her partner smile rather than laugh.

26	A TO Z

Easy

Description: Players will have a conversation that follows the alphabet. Based on a suggestion, players exchange lines in which the first line starts with the letter A, the second line starts with the letter B, and so on. For example: Player A says, "**A**lright, I've got the blankets and the picnic." Player B responds, "**B**etter take my convertible; I'll pop the top." Player A replies, "**C**razy guy, my hair always gets so tangled from the wind." Be careful not to skip any letters. It is acceptable to make up an "X" word such as **X**actly (exactly).

Variations:
1. Follow the alphabet from Z to A. This makes the exercise much more difficult.
2. Begin by going forward in the alphabet. When a third person or the facilitator periodically says "Reverse," go backward in the alphabet, and when he says "Forward," go forward again.

> **Hint:** It is important that the lines form a coherent conversation rather than independent sentences.

Practice being excited.
Bill Foster

78

27	BASIC MIRROR

Easy

Description: One player will reflect the movements of the other. Two players stand face to face about two feet apart. One player slowly moves his body and face, while the other reflects all his movements, including facial expressions. It should look as if the first player is looking into a mirror. Ideally, the movements should be so synchronized that it is difficult to tell who is initiating and who is following the movements. Be sure to note that this is a silent exercise with no talking. Switch leaders after a while.

Hint: The player initiating the movements needs to be aware of how fast he can move through feedback from his partner's movements. If she cannot keep up, he is moving too fast. Remind players that this exercise is about cooperation rather than competition.

Discussion: Ask ❑ What did you learn about non-verbal communication? ❑ How many of you felt connected with your partner after this exercise? ❑ What was easy or difficult about it?

28   TWO SIDED

Easy

Description: Two players will speak as one person. They alternately say one word at a time to form complete sentences. They should speak as fast as possible while trying to make grammatical sense. The facilitator can have players answer simple questions, such as "How do you make a peanut butter sandwich?" Here is an example:

Player A		Player B
First	→	you
open	→	the
jar	→	of
peanut	→	butter
with	→	your
hands.		

Hint: It is important to let go of independent ideas and concentrate on working as a team. The trick is not to think too hard.

Variations:
1. Two pairs of partners have a conversation with each other.
2. With the group divided into two-sided partners (twelve players would equal six two-sided people), the partners go arm-in-arm around the room and have conversations with other two-sided people.

Discussion: Ask ☐ How many different ways are there to make a peanut butter sandwich (or whatever they were talking about)? ☐ How many ways are there to describe things? ☐ What did you have to do to make your answers work? ☐ How many of you had one idea while your partner had another? ☐ How often does this happen in real life? ☐ What can we learn from this exercise? ☐ Was it hard to let go of control?

29	FORBIDDEN LETTER

Medium

Description: Players will have a conversation without using words that begin with a specified letter. The facilitator solicits a consonant in the alphabet from the group. Partners have conversations without using any words that begin with that letter. For example: If the letter is "T", words such as "the", "today", and "there" can't be used.

Variations:
1. Players can't use words that begin with two or more different letters.
2. Players can't use words with a certain number of letters. For example: No three-letter words.
3. Players can't use words that contain a specific vowel. This makes this exercise a real challenge.

30	CHANGES

Medium

Description: Players will study each other, secretly make changes, and then notice what changes the other has made. Partners look at one another for about a minute or so, paying attention to as many details as possible. The facilitator then asks the partners to turn their backs to one another and make four changes on themselves (unbuttoning a button, parting their hair differently, switching their watch to the other arm, etc.). The changes can be very subtle. When everyone is ready, the players turn around and identify the changes their partners have made. Repeat this game as many times as desired, and try seven or as many as ten changes.

> **Hint:** Players might complain when you increase the number of changes because they feel it is too difficult to make and recognize that many changes. When compelled to accept this increase, they will be amazed by how they can adapt.

Discussion: Ask ❏ How much do we really notice about others? ❏ Why are we so reluctant to change?

Only those who dare to fail greatly can ever achieve greatly.
Robert Francis Kennedy

31	SENTENCE STORY

Medium

Description: Players will make up a story in which each player says only half of each sentence. Player A begins a story and stops halfway through the first sentence. Player B immediately finishes that sentence and starts another one. Halfway through that one, it goes back to Player A, and so on. There should be no pause in the transition from one player to the other and eye contact can be very helpful to signify when each player has stopped. The sentences should still be grammatically correct and logically continue the story.

> **Hint**: Focus on making the story move forward and speaking quickly.

Variation: With three players, Player A begins the story by saying the first half of a sentence. Player B then finishes the sentence. Player C starts the second sentence, and Player A completes it, and so on. This can be played with many people, but it should be done with an odd number of people so the players get to alternate between starting and finishing sentences.

The future belongs to those who live intensely in the present.
Anon

32   EMBELLISHMENT

Medium

Description: One player will tell a story based on a suggestion, and another will retell it, embellishing it with details. Player A tells a story, pausing after each line. At each pause, Player B retells that part of the story, adding details that color the story. For example: Player A says, "While running toward the mall, I saw a helicopter fly over the hospital." She pauses and Player B says, "Feeling the dirt beneath my shoes, my knees aching from the five miles I'd just run, I paused to catch my breath. That's when I heard the roar of a helicopter darting overhead, making me feel as though it just missed my head on its way to the hospital landing pad." This continues for a few minutes. The purpose of this exercise is to enhance story telling abilities and to help players appreciate the importance of details.

Hint: This exercise is great for creative writing.

Variations:
1. In a small group, a different player around the circle embellishes each of the storyteller's lines.
2. Add a theme or style to the embellishments, such as an emotion, movie style, geographical location, or age group. (See page 157 for a discussion on endowments and influences.)

Whatever there be of progress in life comes not through adaptation but through daring, through obeying the blind urge.
Henry Miller

33   DIS-EMBELLISHMENT

Medium

Description: In partners, one player takes one minute to tell about an experience or problem that causes them stress or unhappiness in their lives. Then the second player reduces the experience/problem to a short headline. This can help reduce the power that a negative experience has over someone's life, or it can make a problem seem more manageable.

For example: Player A might say "The other day I had to rush to the store because we were out of eggs and I was making a cake. It was awful. The man behind me in line was really rude. He said I had cut in line in front of him, but I didn't. It made me so upset. When I got to the front of the line, I didn't have enough money, so I had to get back out of the line and go to the ATM. That's when I saw my friend Ellen who always looks so perfect. I could tell by the way she said hello that she didn't approve of my messy hair. She's always so judgmental." And she goes on for about a minute. Player B's summary headline might be "Woman goes to the store and brings home eggs."

Variation: This variation is less personal. One player makes up a one-minute story that includes a lot of detail. A second player reduces the story into a single headline.

Everything flows, nothing stays still.
Heraclitus

34	EMOTIONAL ROLLERCOASTER

Medium

Description: Two players have a conversation or tell a story in which the emotion from which they are speaking periodically changes. The facilitator gathers a list of about 10 emotions. Players begin a conversation or story based on a suggestion, and every 10 to 15 seconds, the facilitator shouts out a new emotion from the list. At that time, the other player takes over telling the story or having the conversation with the new emotion. This exercise works best when each emotion called out is very different from the emotion currently being expressed (from happy to sad, etc.).

For example: Player A begins by saying, "The storm was raging and the passengers on board the steam ship were becoming worried. Lisa began to sing to distract herself from the danger, 'Row, row, row your boat...'" The facilitator shouts "SADNESS!" Player B continues the storyline by singing in a sad voice, "...gently down the stream." The facilitator shouts "FRANTIC!" Player A continues the story in a frenzied voice, "...Lisa stopped! She started packing her suitcase, being sure to fold her socks tightly, when she saw her half-finished Red Bull and pounded it." The facilitator shouts "OBNOXIOUS!" Player B continues with "...BURP! She threw the can toward the steward walking by and zipped her suitcase. Noticing a pair of underwear on the floor she pulled them over her head." The facilitator shouts "LOVE!" Player A says, "Her heart pounded as she walked past the steward. Dumbfounded by the bump on his head, he stared into Lisa's eyes. He said, 'Your eyes, they match the underwear you're wearing on your head.'" And this continues until all of the emotions have been used or the facilitator feels the story has reached a logical place to end.

Hint: Remind players to keep the conversation going in the same direction. They should not change the content or "gist" of the conversation or contradict something that was said earlier because they have a different emotion. They should also express the emotion without saying the name of the emotion, and the non-verbal expression of the emotion is as important as the verbal expression.

Discussion: Ask ❏ What happened to the conversation when the emotion changed to _____? (Fill in the blank with various emotions.)

Be like a very small joyous child living in the ever-present now without a single worry or concern about even the next moment of time.

Eileen Caddy

35 LAST LETTER, FIRST LETTER

Medium

Description: Two players will have a conversation in which the *last* letter of one player's line becomes the *first* letter of the other player's next line.

For example: Player A says, "Eli, hand me the pliers." Player B responds, "Sure Noah, looks like you've almost got it." Player A says, "Thanks, you helped a lot". Player B answers, "Take it easy; it was no big deal."

> **Hint:** Players should keep the conversation moving forward.

36 SCRIPTORAMA

Medium

Description: Each pair will interpret a basic script in a different way. This exercise requires significantly more time than the other exercises. Prior to the exercise, the facilitator makes enough copies of the basic script on the next page for each pair in the group, or writes a new short two-people script and makes copies of it. The script should consist of simple, non-specific lines of dialogue. After each pair is given a copy of the script, they are given time to determine the *who, what* and *where* of the script and to develop and practice their scenes. Then they should return and present their scenes to the group. The details of the scene are filled in by the way the players interact with each other and their imaginary environment (see page 153 for a discussion of miming and *who, what* and *where*). If the group is too large for every pair to present, select a few volunteer pairs. Every pair must follow the script word for word, but they can present it in any way they wish with any context they determine.

Hint: Have the partners present their scenes and allow the group to guess the who, what, and where. Remind the actors to use solid, interesting and believable characters in their scenes.

Variation: Two players improvise the same script in many different ways with unlimited possibilities.

Discussion: ❑ Talk about how the same script can lead to an unlimited number of possibilities. ❑ Discuss the influence non-verbal forms of communication had on differences between the scenes.

SAMPLE BASIC SCRIPT

Player A: Look at that.

Player B: Holy cow.

Player A: We should go.

Player B: I'll get it.

Player A: Two more and we're done.

Player B: Here you go.

37   WHAT ARE YOU DOING?

Medium

Description: Two players will mime one activity while claiming to do another. Player A begins by miming any activity, like brushing her teeth. After three to five seconds, Player B asks, "What are you doing?" Player A names an activity that is different from the one she is currently miming, such as playing a violin. Player B then mimes playing a violin. Then Player A asks, "What are you doing?" Player B must say anything other than an activity that resembles playing a violin.

The challenge of this exercise is doing one activity while saying you are doing something totally unrelated. It is similar to patting your head while rubbing your stomach. This goes back and forth until one player makes a mistake by saying an activity that has already been done, saying an activity that resembles what he is currently acting out, or hesitating. Each player should allow the other player to mime an activity for a few seconds before asking, "What are you doing?" Increase the speed as the game progresses.

Hint: Urge players to really do the activity and give 100%.

Variation: This can be played as a line game with the next player in line replacing the player who made a mistake.

Discussion: Ask ❑ What was difficult about this exercise? ❑ Did you really *do* the activities?

---

38   SWITCHING MIRROR

Medium

Description: This exercise is like **BASIC MIRROR** on page 79, except the facilitator calls out "Switch" every 10 seconds and the control switches from one player to the other. The switch of control should be immediate and the flow of the movement should be continuous. After calling out switch a few times, the facilitator can call out "Both" and at this time both players reflect each other's movements simultaneously. This is difficult because the partners must reflect themselves being reflected.

Hint: Tell the partners that you should not be able to tell who is initiating the movement and who is following.

Discussion: Ask ❑ How many pairs were synchronized? ❑ Why or why not? ❑ Did you prefer leading or following? Why?

39   YES, AND . . . NO, BUT . . .

Medium

Description: Partners will have three conversations in which the dialogue of both players is limited. One player begins every round with the same phrase that is a suggestion. For example: "Let's go have a burger." From then on, both players must begin each line of dialog with one of three statements. For the first minute, or so, both players' responses must start with "No…, but…." In the second conversations, the initial suggestion is repeated, and for the next minute, each reply must start with "Yes…, but…." Finally, in the third conversation, the players will transition to start their responses with "Yes…, and…."

For example: In response to "Let's go have a burger," Player B might respond with, "No, I don't like burgers, but we could go have pizza." Player A might reply "No, you always choose pizza, but today I get to choose," and so on. Next, each response must contain "Yes…, but…." In the same example player B might say "Yes, a burger sounds good, but I'll drive to the burger joint." Player A might respond "Yes, you can drive, but I get to steer," and so on. The last time through, both partners reply with "Yes…, and…." In this example player B might respond "Yes, I love burgers, and we can have five each." Then Player B might say "Yes, and we can bring my grandmother with us."

Variations:
1. Only one player's replies are restricted. The first player is free to say anything he wants.
2. Start with a mundane topic, like the burger example above. Then make the first statement a real and pertinent issue, such as, "America needs more governmental regulations," or "Let's give everyone a raise."

Discussion: Doing this exercise is a good way to really understand the difference between "No, but," "Yes, but" and "Yes, and." Ask ☐ How did it feel when someone said "Yes, and…"? ☐ How did it feel when they said "Yes, but…"? ☐ How about "No, but…"? ☐ What did you notice about the energy in the various conversations?

40　　　RHYME LINES

Medium

Description: Two players will have a conversation in which every two lines rhyme. Player A says a line and Player B replies with a line that rhymes with the first. Then, Player B says a second line that Player A must respond to with a rhyming line. This pattern ensures one player is not always stuck with the job of rhyming. This goes back and forth until one of the players cannot come back with a rhyming line. Players should try to keep the lengths of the lines consistent, like in a poem.

For Example: Player A says, "Looks like we'll have to take off the door." Player B replies, "I'll give you a hand; it's really no chore." Then Player B sends Player A another line, such as, "Here we go; ouch, I hurt my back!" Player B might say "Set it down next to my Big Mac."

> **Hint:** Ask players to avoid ending lines with words that are difficult to rhyme with, such as orange and Australia.

Variation: This can be done as a duet singing activity with two people making up a song together. In a song, the lines don't necessarily need to be a conversation.

Humorists can never start to take themselves seriously. It's literary suicide.

Erma Bombeck

41   FIRST AND LAST

Medium

Description: Players will have a conversation with a predetermined first and last line. The facilitator gets two lines of unrelated dialogue from the group. Player A starts the conversation with one of the lines. Player B responds to that line with a suitable line. The two players continue the conversation until it becomes appropriate in the context of the conversation to end with the second line of dialogue. The two lines can be two random lines or lines from different songs, advertisement slogans, or unrelated news headlines, etc.

For example: If the two lines were "Just do it" and "Where's the beef?" the conversation might go like this...

> **Player A:** Where's the beef?
>
> **Player B:** In the fridge next to the salad.
>
> **Player A:** Ick! It's disgustingly moldy.
>
> **Player B:** Throw it out then. We can't eat it.
>
> **Player A:** But it was so expensive.
>
> **Player B:** Just do it!

Hint: Don't force the second line too soon. It should sound natural.

Variations:
1. Players must use the last line within a limited or specified number of exchanges, such as eight or ten.
2. Partners or individuals write a very short story with one of the lines as the first line and the other line as the last line of the story.

42   GIBBERISH LESSONS

Medium

Description: Players will learn a new language. Gibberish is a fun, made-up language that is used in several exercises and games. It is the substitution of varied sounds for recognizable words. When players speak Gibberish, they use familiar sounds or parts of words that sound like a real language. "Shav basod cronk suf lezo" is an example of Gibberish. "Blah blah blah blah" is not. There should be distinctive intonations and articulation instead of unconvincing grunts. The facilitator can demonstrate Gibberish by saying, "Repeat after me. Subu stoe tanka tap muck po." Then the partners should practice by having conversations in this new made-up language. Players should conduct themselves as if they know exactly what they are saying.

43   LANGUAGE BARRIER

Medium

Description: Two players will have a conversation in which one person speaks in Gibberish (see **GIBBERISH LESSONS** above) while the other speaks in English. The players should switch roles periodically.

Discussion: Ask ❑ How did it feel? ❑ What did you notice? ❑ Were you still able to communicate?

Trust thyself: every heart vibrates to that iron string.
Ralph Waldo Emerson

44   UP AND DOWN

Hard

Description: The players will have a conversation in which the sentences get longer and then shorter. The lengths of the sentences in the conversation progress in length from one word to five words and then back down from five words to one word.

For example:

Player A	Player B
"Hi!"	"Hello Lesha!"
"You look great."	"Thanks, I feel great."
"I've been working out myself?"	"I've seen you running."
"By the river?"	"Last Friday"
"Cool"	

The conversation can end there or it can continue on in the same way.

Hint: Focus on moving the conversation along coherently.

Variation: Both players start with a one-word sentence, then both say a two-word sentence, and so on.

45	COUNTDOWN

Hard

Description: Players will have a conversation or act out a mini-scene in which all of the words are numbers. Select a number between 5 and 20. Larger numbers result in longer conversations, and smaller numbers lead to shorter conversations. The players then have a conversation in which they say one number at a time beginning with the highest and counting down to zero. The players do not simply count backwards. They add intonations, facial expressions and pauses that add meaning.

For example: If the number is 12, a conversation might go like this. Player A starts by saying "12," in a way that conveys some meaning, such as with a questioning intonation. Player B responds with "11." He might say it shyly, or with a pause and in an irritated tone. Some other possible variations are to express frustration, conflict, excitement, shame, questioning, or surprise.

This exercise illustrates that it is not just *what* you say, but *how* you say it that matters. It's fun to bring several pairs to the front of the group to demonstrate their interpretations of the numbers conversation. This helps show the group the many different ways the same words can be expressed.

> **Hint:** Ask the observers to guess what the number conversation was about. There is, of course, no right or wrong answer here and the two players involved might have totally different answers.

Variation: The group sets up a scenario before the conversation starts, such as an interaction at a post office or a used car sales lot. Roles can be assigned to the players. Then try the same scenario a second time with normal dialogue.

Discussion: Ask ☐ Could you guess specifically what they were saying? ☐ How much of our communication with others is about how we say something, not what we say? ❑ What did you notice about the conversation when you knew it would end after a specific number of interactions? ❑ How did that affect the conversation?

46	FIXED WORD

Hard

Description: Players will have a conversation in which each sentence has a specified number of words. The group chooses a number from two to six. Then two or three players have a conversation based on a suggestion, in which each line of dialogue must have the chosen number of words.

For example: If the number is four, Player A might say, "The sunset is beautiful." Player B responds, "Yes, it really is." Player A says, "Let's take a walk." Player B says, "Boy, I'd love to." This is a challenging and fun way to communicate.

Hint: Advise players to avoid asking questions.

Variation: The number of syllables in each sentence is specified (extremely difficult).

47	SLIDING MIRROR

Hard

Description: In this **MIRROR** exercise, as the facilitator slowly counts from 1 to 10 out loud, the degree of control gradually shifts from one player to the other. Two players act as a mirror (see **BASIC MIRROR** on page 79). At "1", Player A is in total control, and by "10", Player B is in total control. By the count of "4" Player A is barely in control and at "5" neither player is in control. They are both reacting to each other's movements and they might feel weird, but there should still be movement. At "6" Player B begins taking control and by "10" Player B is in total control. In other words, the numbers "2" through "8" are a gradual transition of control. Each player is partly controlling and partly reacting. Who is directing the movements is ambiguous to everyone, but there are still movements happening. The facilitator can say more than just the number. For example: With the number "4" the facilitator could say "Now player A is barely in control."

> **Hint:** This is a terrific exercise to use when discussing leadership. Count slowly and remind them that this is a silent exercise. Players may have a hard time around "4" through "6", but this is where there can be some interesting experiences that lead to terrific discussions. Often neither player feels he is causing the movements in this zone.

Discussion: Ask ❒ What was difficult about this exercise? ❒ How many of you preferred to be in control? Why? ❒ Did either player prefer to follow? Why? ❒ What did it feel like at the count of "4", "5", and "6"? ❒ What happened at "5"? ❒ When is it appropriate to be in total control? ❒ When is it appropriate to let another person lead?

48 FUNKY MIRROR

Hard

Description: In this MIRROR exercise, neither player is in control, but there is still movement. This whole exercise is like being at "5" in SLIDING MIRROR (opposite page). There is no leader and no follower the whole time, but the facilitator ought to clarify that there should still be movement. Both the players doing the exercise and the people watching shouldn't be able to tell who is initiating the movement. As the title suggests, this exercise is funky, but give it a try. It can lead to some interesting discussion.

> **Hint:** Reinforce the point that there must be movement and that you shouldn't be able to tell by watching who is initiating a movement and who is responding. If you let this run for a while it becomes like a dance.

Mirth is like a flash of lightning, that breaks through a gloom of clouds, and glitters for a moment; cheerfulness keeps up a kind of daylight in the mind, and fills it with a steady and perpetual serenity.

Joseph Addison

49	GIBBERISH SWITCH

Hard

Description: Two players will have a conversation that switches between English and Gibberish. The players start a conversation in English that is based on a suggestion. When the facilitator claps once (or yells "Switch") after 10 to 15 seconds, the conversation switches to Gibberish (see GIBBERISH LESSONS on page 95). At the next clap it switches back to English, and so on. It is important that the conversation moves forward while Gibberish is being spoken. The things said in Gibberish should be addressed when the conversation changes back to English.

For example: Player A says, "So while we were at the game, I ordered this hot dog and the vender guy said, 'What do you want on it?' Well of course being on a diet I said, just ketchup." Player B replies, "Yeah, so he put ketchup on it, big deal." Player A returns with, "Well this is the funny part. Not only…" CLAP (the clapper claps once). Without stopping her conversation, Player A immediately continues with, "…bla sta bo lamotosta a nocko." Player B says, with an understanding expression, "Ca, sta po pla zimiki. Yo sta cuco esbo cha tae." Player A might return with, "Shaa toto makosta lova…" CLAP …hands to wipe up the ketchup, and then he drops his tray of hot dogs…." This continues with the clapper clapping at the most opportune times, which may be right after a transition in the story.

> **Hint:** A lot of gesturing and facial expressions should be used with Gibberish. Many people begin "denying" when they switch to Gibberish. They resist accepting something in the unknown, so players should avoid saying "no" or gesturing no. It is important to say "yes" and gesture yes.

Discussion: Ask ❐ What did you notice when you switched to Gibberish? ❐ How did the energy change? ❐ Was it hard to continue the flow of the conversation?

50   ONLY QUESTIONS

Hard

Description: The players will have a conversation in which the entire dialogue is spoken in questions. For example: Player A says, "Can you help with the pancakes?" Player B responds, "Are you implying you knew my college nickname, 'The Flipper?'" Player A replies, "Are you kidding? Your reputation lives on.... some meat?" Player B continues with, "Didn't you know I am a vegetarian?" Player A, "Did you stop eating meat because your boyfriend is a health nut?"

Discussion: Ask ❏ Can you do this exercise without confrontation?

I remain just one thing, and one thing only—and that is a clown.
It places me on a far higher plane than any politician.
                 Charlie Chaplin

51   TALKING MIRROR

Hard

Description: One player will reflect the other player's speaking and movements. This is like BASIC MIRROR on page 79 with speaking added to the movements. One player begins speaking slowly and enunciating carefully while the other player tries to simultaneously speak out loud what the initiator says. Movements should be very simple.

> **Hint:** This exercise causes a lot of self-consciousness and may create enormous spontaneous laughter. It is one of the most whacky and "in-your-face" exercises and can be loads of fun.

Variations:
1. The facilitator claps every 5 to 10 seconds at which time the control switches from one player to the other.
2. A third player tries to guess who is leading and who is following. The two players mirroring each other should work together to fool the observer.

Discussion: Ask ❏ What was easier, leading or following? ❏ Could someone watching the partners tell who was leading and who was following? (This *should* be difficult, but it will be obvious who is leading and who is following in some pairs.) ❏ Is it easier to be the leader or the follower? Why?

52   SING IT

Hard

Description: The players will have a singing conversation. This is quite straightforward, but it can be difficult for some people. The conversation is normal except the players sing the words instead of speaking them. Players make up the melodies as they go along and the lines do not need to rhyme.

> **Hint:** Urge the players to give 100%.

Variations:

1. Choose a style of music such as country western, opera, or rap.

2. Use this exercise as a communication workshop. For example: Have participants resolve a conflict while singing, or hold a meeting where everyone must sing.

Discussion: Ask ❏ Can you imagine how carefully we'd choose our responses at the next company meeting if everyone was singing? ❏ What would happen if you turned your next family meeting into a family opera?

Risk! Risk anything! Care no more for the opinion of others, for those voices. Do the hardest thing on earth for you. Act for yourself.

Katherine Mansfield

53	BACK TALK

Hard

Description: The players will speak the sentences of a conversation in reverse order. The words in each sentence are spoken in the correct order; only the order of the sentences is reversed. For example: Player A starts by saying, "All right then, lets just hang it here." Player B now must think of a line of dialogue that could precede that statement. Player B might say, "I don't like how the picture looks on this wall." Player A then has to think of a line that could precede that line such as, "Here we go, right next to the Monet."

Hint: Have a third person jot down the lines while they are being spoken and reverse them at the end to see if the conversation made logical sense. Advise players to avoid asking questions.

Variations:
1. At the end (or is it the beginning?), the players say the conversation forward.
2. Play this exercise like the game FORWARD/REVERSE (see page 182). A third player says "forward" or "reverse," and the two speaking players follow the commands accordingly.

54	FIVE LETTER WORD

Hard

Description: Players will have a conversation in which each line begins with a letter from a five-letter word. The facilitator gets a suggestion of a five-letter word from the group. Then the players use the letters from the chosen word (in order) as the first letters of lines of dialogue in a conversation.

For example: If the word is "house," a conversation between two players might sound like this.

Player A: "Hi mom."

Player B: "Oh boy, Terry, it's so good to see you."

Player A: "Usually I'm not this late."

Player B: "Son, don't worry about it."

Player A: "Every time I'm late you're so nice about it."

The conversation can stop here, or it can be continued by repeating the same sequence of letters.

Variation: This game can also be played with three- or seven-letter words.

55   EMOTIONAL SEESAW

Hard

Description: Two players will have a conversation in which they periodically trade emotions. Two players start a conversation (based on a suggestion) with opposite emotions, such as happy and sad, or excited and bored. When the facilitator says "switch" every ten seconds or so, the players switch their respective emotions. It is important that the context of the conversation continue when the emotions are switched. The players should not actually say the name of their assigned emotion; they should just take on that emotion and maintain the central idea of the conversation.

Variations:
1. Players are assigned styles other than emotions, such as movie styles, ages, or nationalities (see page 157 for a discussion on endowments and influences).
2. Players are assigned opposite personality types, such as a controlling person vs. a subservient person, pompous vs. humble, or sensitive vs. insensitive.

56 MID-WORD STORY

Hard

Description: Partners or small groups will tell a story by finishing each other's words and sentences. The first player starts a story (based on a suggestion) in third person, saying something like, "Don was walking..." rather than "I was walking...." After five to ten seconds, she stops in the middle of the word she is starting to say, and the next player quickly continues the story by finishing the previous player's unfinished word. The twist, however, is that the next player should not finish the word the previous player had in mind. The new word must combine with the original word's beginning to form a real word that continues the story.

For example: If Player A said, "....Joe was running to catch up with the other kids, when he tripped over a ro...".rather than responding with the obvious choice of rock, Player B could say, "...cket ship that NASA had lost track of three days earlier," and continue from there. The next line could be something like, "Just then the other kids saw what looked like a Martian crawling out of the rocket ship and yelled, 'GET UP J...'". Instead of finishing with the obvious "Joe," the other player might say "...oyfully, so the Martian doesn't think you're scared."

> **Hint:** Remind players to enunciate well. Also, emphasize that they need to justify the new word in the story. In other words, if they say a new word it should enhance the story and be included into the flow of the story rather than being said only once and not ever addressed again.

CHAPTER 10

SMALL GROUP EXERCISES

THIS CHAPTER INCLUDES exercises for groups of 4 to 12. These exercises all provide various benefits such as improving attention to detail, conflict resolution skills and non-verbal communication (see Appendix E). They typically last longer than the exercises for partners and they can be used to make some great points.

57	OH NO

Easy

Description: Players stand in a circle looking at the floor. On the count of three, everyone looks up at either the person on their right, on their left, or directly across from them. If that person is looking back, both go "oh no" and step out of the circle. This continues until only two people are left.

58   AIR JUMP

Easy

Description: Teams will play a game of jump rope with an imaginary rope. In teams of four to six, each team plays its own game of jump rope using an imaginary rope. Some players turn the rope while the other players jump or watch. Players should be rotated until everyone has had a chance to turn the rope and jump.

> **Hint:** Encourage players to really "see" the rope, focus, and to commit 100% to the activity. Although this is an easy exercise, people might be reluctant to play.

Discussion: Ask ❐ What made this exercise work? ❐ Did it look to the observers like there really was a jump rope? ❐ Were you really focused?

59   SHAPE UP

Easy

Description: Players stand in a circle and hold hands, and the facilitator asks them to form shapes as a group, such as a perfect square, circle, rectangle, or diamond, without letting go of hands.

Variations:
1. Players make shapes first with their eyes closed, then without speaking, and finally, with both closed eyes and without speaking.
2. As a group, players make objects such as an airplane, a bridge, or a building. Players don't have to hold hands in this variation. Encourage them to let their creativity flow.

60   ALL TALK

Easy

Description: All players will talk to someone while listening to someone else. In a circle, players turn toward the person on their right and on the count of three tell them how to play their favorite sport, make their favorite dinner or anything else. The players will be both speaking to the person on their right and listening to the person on their left at the same time.

> **Hint:** This is pretty hard to do and demonstrates the difficulty of talking and listening at the same time. Use this when the group begins to talk while they should be listening.

Variation: Players try to maintain a conversation with both people.

Discussion: Ask ❑ How many of you were able to speak and listen at the same time?

61	CLEAR CATCH

Easy

Description: Players will toss an imaginary basketball to each other. With the group standing in a circle, one player begins by throwing the imaginary basketball to another player. The thrower should toss the imaginary basketball in a way that another player could catch it, using strong miming techniques. After a while, the players should "see" the ball and it should look like they are really tossing around a basketball.

> **Hint:** Have the players toss the "ball" around faster and faster, which will cause the group to become more and more focused.

Variation: Replace the basketball with a softball, balloon, Frisbee, hot potato, etc.

62   CONVERSATION CHAOS

Easy

Description: Players will have simultaneous conversations with the person across from them in a circle. This exercise requires an even number of players. The players form a circle and make eye contact with the person directly across from them who will be their conversation partner. Choose a topic for the conversations. With the players remaining in the circle, the facilitator counts to three and the conversations across the circle begin. The players' objective is to keep the conversations going with their partners even though there are several other conversations going on around them.

> **Hint:** After the game has been played for a little while, tell the group, "This time, focus not only on trying to communicate with your partner, but also on ensuring that everyone else in the group can communicate with their partners."

Variations:
1. The players talk softly.
2. The players close their eyes and continue conversing. Notice what happens to the conversations.

Discussion: Ask ❑ What made it easy or hard to communicate with your partner? ❑ What happened to the group? ❑ What was distracting? ❑ What can we learn about communicating from this exercise?

63 PASS THE ENERGY

Easy

Description: Players will "pass" each other a changing shape of energy. In a circle, the first player holds an imaginary ball of energy. Her job is to hand this ball of energy to the next player. This player then takes the ball of energy, transforms it in any way he wants, and passes it on to the next player. The energy can be stretched, smashed, flattened, added to, made heavier or light as a feather, or altered in any other way. It is important for each player to accept the energy in the shape it is handed to him and change the shape only after it is accepted.

Hint: Encourage players not to hold back while altering the energy. It is amazing how creative some people will be with this exercise.

Variation: Tell the group that the energy represents something, such as their stress, the way they are currently feeling, the thing that is most important to them, or the culture of the organization.

64 PASS THE CLAP

Easy

Description: Players will "pass" a clap randomly around a circle. One person claps and passes that clap to someone else. That person reaches out, grabs the clap and brings it toward him (as if he is catching the passed clap) and then passes a clap to a different person. The passer should make eye contact with the person he is tossing the clap to. Speed it up for extra fun.

Humour is by far the most significant activity of the human brain.

Edward De Bono

65   PASS THE MASK

Easy

Description: Players will "pass" strange faces around a circle. A designated player turns to the player on his right, looks into her eyes and makes an unusual face (the "mask"). The second player passes this face on to the third player, and so on around the circle. Immediately after passing the first mask, the first player turns to the player on his left and makes a different face, which is passed around in that direction. This continues until both masks reach the first player again.

> **Hint:** Ask players to pass the mask around as fast as possible.

Variation: The first player passes a mask to anyone in the circle. That player makes the same mask back and then passes a different mask to someone else.

66   PASS THE MOVEMENT

Easy

Description: Players will "pass" movements around a circle. The first player turns to the player on his right and does a body movement such as touching his elbow to his opposite knee. The second player then repeats the movement to the first player and passes a different movement to the next player in the circle, and so on around the circle.

> **Hint:** Encourage players to focus on repeating the movement rather than on what new movement they will perform. The fun comes from acting spontaneously and initiating the first movement that comes to mind. It is also very important that they make solid eye contact with the person to whom they are passing a sound or movement.

Variations:
1. The movement is replaced with a strange sound, or a combination of a sound and a movement.
2. The first player makes eye contact with a random player in the circle and does a body movement. The player with whom she made eye contact maintains eye contact and repeats her movement. The second player then makes eye contact with another random player and does a new body movement. The third player must return the movement and then pass another one to someone else, and so on.

Our brightest blazes of gladness are commonly kindled by unexpected sparks.

Samuel Johnson

67	PASS THE GAS

Easy

Description: Players will "pass" gas in as many different pitches as they can. In a circle, the first player passes gas in his preferred pitch. The next player tries to make the pitch of the gas she passes higher or lower. This continues around the circle until no one can create a new pitch, or someone fails to pass gas. Players are also eliminated for passing gas at a pitch that has already been created. That is just bad form and shows a complete lack of creativity.

> **Hint:** Eat foods with a lot of natural fiber such as pinto beans and broccoli the night before doing this exercise. This exercise is best done outdoors or in a well-ventilated area.

Variation: Vary the lengths of the gas that is passed rather than the pitch.

Discussion: Ask ❑ What was difficult about this exercise? ❑ How did it feel when your neighbor passed gas?

I remain just one thing, and one thing only—and that is a clown.
It places me on a far higher plane than any politician.

Charlie Chaplin

68 CIRCULAR MIRROR

Easy

Description: Players will reflect the movements of another player. In a circle, a designated player starts by doing a repetitive movement, usually with his arms. Then the rest of the group reflects that movement. After all players are doing the movement in unison, the next player in the circle makes a small change to the movement. Control of the movement continues around the circle each time the group begins to move in unison.

> **Hint:** It is important that players do the movement at the same speed as the leader.

Variations:
1. The player initiating the movement can also add a sound, and when all the other players are doing the same sound and movement, control switches to the next player.
2. One player moves away from the group where he cannot see or hear what is happening in the group. While that player is gone, a leader is designated. The leader begins and changes movements every five seconds or so while the others try to follow. While the group is in motion, the absent player comes back and tries to guess who is initiating the movements. Players should avoid staring at the initiator to avoid pointing her out in that way.

69   THANKS FOR THE . . .

Easy

Description: One player will give another player a mimed imaginary object that the receiver will then name. Objects can be big, small, heavy, light, square, cylindrical, have lids that screw on, etc. For example: Player A picks up an imaginary object and hands it to Player B and says, "Here you go Joy. This is for you." Player B takes the object and says, "Thank you Lee for the _____" and names the object anything she wants as long as it agrees with the shape of the object handed to her. She should briefly, interact with the object, set it down, and then mime grabbing a new object and handing it to the next person in the circle. The receiving player should be specific in identifying the object. For example, he should say "Thanks for the electric blender" rather than "Thanks for the box." This exercise can easily be played with only two players.

> **Hint:** Try to hand the other player an object that is very different from the one you just received. The most important part of this exercise is that the accepting player says "Thank you for the _____," rather than saying, "I don't know what it is," or asking "What is it?" There are no right or wrong answers, and it's not important that the receiving player name the object what the giving player intended it to be; in fact the giving player can respond with "That's exactly what it is", after every description.

Discussion: The vagueness of this exercise makes it difficult for some people. People want to know what the right answer is or what the giving player intended the object to be. Ask ❐ What made this difficult? ❐ How did it feel when your partner named the object something different than what you intended?

70   EMOTIONAL LINE

Easy

Description: Players will say the same phrase with different emotions. The facilitator gets a suggestion for a line of dialogue from the group, and the players are each assigned a different emotion. The players then take turns saying the suggested line of dialogue with their given emotions. This exercise illustrates how it is not just *what* you say, but *how* you say it that matters. This can be done with four volunteers in front of a large group.

71   PLAYGROUND

Easy

Description: Players will play a playground activity without any equipment. The players choose a playground activity such as baseball, basketball, keep-away, or volleyball. Then they play that game with an imaginary ball and/or equipment. They must follow all of the rules of the chosen game.

> **Hint:** Urge players to make it believable, to really "see" the ball, and to commit 100% to the exercise.

Discussion: Ask ❐ How many of you were really committed? ❐ Did you feel that others were committed? ❐ Discuss the difference between doing this exercise with 100% commitment and just going through the motions. Apply this to daily life.

72   WALKA BEEK

Easy

Description: One at a time and in a clockwise direction, each player in a circle says "walka" until a random player says "beek." When someone says "beek," the direction changes and "walka" is now said in a counter-clockwise direction until another player says "beek." If a player does not respond quickly when the direction is reversed, he is eliminated and must leave the circle. This exercise should be played as fast as possible.

73   RHYTHM CIRCLE

Easy

Description: Players will each contribute to a rhythm. The group forms a circle, either sitting or standing. One player starts a simple rhythm using her body and/or voice (clapping her hands, stomping her foot, or vocalizing "beep", etc.), and she keeps that rhythm going for the duration of the exercise. The other players remain quiet until their turn. After about 10 seconds, the next player in the circle adds a new rhythm that complements the first rhythm. In turn, each player adds a unique part to the rhythm. Once everyone is involved and the rhythm has been "played" for a while, the facilitator can instruct the group to speed it up or slow it down.

Every child is an artist. The problem is how to remain an artist once he grows up.

Pablo Picasso

74   THAT'S A GREAT IDEA

Easy

Description: Players will generate ideas and enthusiastically support each other's ideas. First the facilitator has the players practice saying "That's a great idea!" with 100% commitment and enthusiasm. Don't begin the exercise until the group is really into saying it. Then establish a simple and wacky brainstorming topic, such as finding new uses for a lettuce leaf or how to avoid washing dishes. Sitting in a circle, players generate ideas for the goal in rotation and everyone responds to each suggestion by saying "That's a great idea!" with 100% conviction. The emphasis should be on the reinforcement from the group rather than on the practicality or appropriateness of the ideas that are generated. A ridiculous idea that makes no sense whatsoever should get the same response as a brilliant idea. After one or two warm-up goals, solutions should be generated for a real and important goal that is appropriate to the group, such as ways to clean up the earth or increase the money earned by the company in the next year.

> **Hint:** Direct the group to put their energy into saying "that's a great idea" rather than thinking of solutions. In order to prevent players from filtering or blocking the ideas that come into their heads, ask small groups to generate a large number of ideas in a relatively short amount of time with quantity stressed over quality. Emphasize the fact that even silly ideas can lead to great ideas.

Variation: The facilitator gets an unusual object from the group (something from a purse, an umbrella, pocket knife, etc.) and the players brainstorm ways in which the object could be a new invention to be used in a specific setting, such as in the kitchen, in our cars, or at work.

Discussion: Ask ❑ Was it easier to come up with ideas in this exercise than in a normal situation? ❑ How was it when everyone said "That's a great idea!" no matter what you said?

75   FREEZE EASY

Easy

Description: Players will periodically rotate in and out of a scene. Two players start a scene based on a suggestion (see page 155 for a discussion on scenes). After about 10 to 15 seconds, the next player in rotation shouts "freeze," at which time both players freeze as statues in whatever position they are in. The player who shouted steps into either role, takes on that exact character and continues the scene from that point. After another short period of time the next player in line shouts freeze and replaces one of the players. This continues until all players have been in the scene.

Happiness is a function of accepting what is.
                     Werner Erhard

76 WALK AND ROLL

Easy

Description: Each player will create a unique way of crossing the room that the other players will imitate. All players form a line against one wall so they are facing the opposite wall. The first player walks (crawls, slithers, jumps, etc.) across the room in any manner she wishes (with a repeated pattern rather than a bunch of random movements). Then the rest of the group mimics her "walk." When the entire group has crossed the room (either individually or as a group), the next player leads the group back across the room with a different walk. The exercise continues until each player has created a new walk and has had his or her walk adopted by the other players. The last players have the greatest pressure to come up with unique ways of crossing. This exercise should be done without talking or making other noises.

Hint: The emphasis should be on replicating the exact movements of each leader. Urge players to copy each walk as precisely as possible.

Variations:

1. Players divide into groups of two or three who work together to create a way to cross the room. Each crossing is then copied by the other groups.

2. Players walk across the room as a specific character, such as a muscle-bound man, a shy girl or an elated old woman.

3. Every player goes across only once without the other repeating their walk. This variation takes a lot less time.

77	SLOW MO TAG

Easy

Description: Players will play a traditional game of tag in slow motion. Designate boundaries for the game in an area that is free of obstacles. A player is chosen to be "it." "It" moves in slow motion while trying to catch the other players as they run, duck, lunge, laugh, etc., in very slow motion. Even the facial expressions of players should be in slow motion. When the "it" player tags another player, the tagged player becomes "it."

> **Hint:** Remind players that they are responsible for moving at the same speed as the other players.

Variation: When players are tagged, they must freeze. The "it" player continues tagging other players until everyone is frozen. The untagged players must stay within the given boundaries and move in slow motion between and around frozen players.

78	MIME A ROOM

Medium

Description: Each player will identify a specific location through miming so that the others can guess where they are. Players form a line facing the stage area (about eight feet by eight feet). One by one they open an imaginary door, enter a location and interact with imaginary objects so that the viewing players can guess where they are. The performing player should imagine the room and the objects in it before opening the door. The space can be inside (kitchen, grocery store) or outside (playground, forest). No talking or sound effects are allowed.

Variations:
1. The facilitator whispers an activity and location into each player's ear before they enter the space and interact with it. For example: "Planting a garden on a mountain slope." Each player can stop when the other players guess the activity and location.
2. The first player goes through the door and interacts with only one item (drinks from a cup) then walks out the other side. The next player goes through the door, interacts with a new item (takes a knife out of a drawer and sharpens it) and then interacts with the item the previous player interacted with (puts the cup into the sink). Each additional player adds a new item then interacts with all the previous items. This can continue until each player has had a turn, or it can continue on with players being eliminated when they miss an item.

79 EXAGGERATE, WHINE, SEE THE GOOD SIDE

Medium

Description: Three players will provide three different perspectives on a problem. The facilitator gets a suggestion for a common issue that many people complain about. One player exaggerates about it, a second whines about it, and a third player focuses on the good side. A fourth player acts as the conductor and controls who is speaking by pointing at one, two, or all three players. Players can only talk when the conductor points to them. They do not have a conversation with each other but deliver independent monologues from their perspective.

For example: If the issue is the length of a school day, the exaggerating player might say, "The school day is so long that I don't have time to sleep," the whining player might whine, "My butt hurts when I have to sit so long," and the good-side player might declare, "The longer I'm in school each day, the more I can learn."

Hint: This exercise can be performed in front of a large group to illustrate the effect of different ways of perceiving a problem.

80	GRAB A BAG

Medium

Description: The group will tell a story that incorporates the items in a bag. The group gathers a bunch of small items, puts them into a bag, and sits in a circle. The first player begins a story that incorporates an item he grabs from the bag. The items can be incorporated into the story literally or can influence it subtly. For example: If the item was a ruler, the story teller could say, "He took out his *ruler*, measured the room, and found it was exactly six feet by six feet," or he could say, "He *inched* his way forward and peeped through the hole." After a few sentences, he passes the bag to the next player who also grabs an item and incorporates it into the story. This continues until the bag is empty or the story is finished.

> **Hint:** Remind the players that the story should make sense. The items should not change what has already happened in the story. Subtle influences by the items make it easier to maintain the story's integrity.

My way of joking is to tell the truth. It's the funniest joke in the world.

George Bernard Shaw

81	ADD A PART

Medium

Description: Players will identify an object by acting on parts of it. The first player thinks of a large object (such as a car) without telling anyone what it is. He then acts as if he is using or contacting a part of that object (sitting and turning the steering wheel, opening the door, etc.). When another player thinks she knows what the object is, she begins to contact or use another part in some way (wiping the windshield). Players can interact with the object and then walk away when another player begins to act on the it. One by one, players use or contact other parts of the object until the whole object is identified or everyone has interacted with the object.

Discussion: Ask ❏ What object were you acting on?

82	GROUP EFFORT

Medium

Description: Teams will work together to move an imaginary object. In teams of three to eight players, each team selects an imaginary object they can move or use together. Then they participate in a joint action in which all move or use the object. For example: They might act as if they are pulling a fishnet, portaging a canoe, or carrying a huge log. The focus should be on teamwork, and the movements should look realistic and coordinated. This is possible only when the team members visualize the object they are moving and are aware of the size, shape, and weight of the object as well as the movements of other team members. Observers will be able to tell if they are truly working as a team and should try to guess what the object is.

| 83 | HITCHHIKER |

Medium

Description: Three players will take on the characteristics of a fourth player. Four chairs are arranged as an imaginary car with two chairs in front and two in back. Four players go on a trip in the car and a designated player is the first to speak and act. This player is a distinctive character (an old lady, a surfer dude, etc.) with some obvious characteristics (a southern accent, a nervous habit, etc.). The other three people in the car attempt to take on the characteristics of the first player and continue the conversation. When all have taken on the characteristics and each has said a line of dialogue, a hitchhiker is picked up and takes the place of one of the players in the car. The hitchhiker is a new character (shy young girl, whiny little boy, etc.) and everyone in the car now must take on the traits of the new person while continuing the original conversation. New hitchhikers should rotate in about every 30 seconds.

When the first hitchhiker is picked up, the driver moves out of the car, the front passenger slides over and starts to drive, and the hitchhiker sits in the front passenger seat. The next hitchhiker sits in the back, the person behind the driver gets out, and the other player in back slides over. The hitchhikers should alternately sit in the front and back until each player has established his own character and taken on the characters of three other players. This exercise flows smoother if the players justify their entrances and exits from the car by saying something like "Here's my stop. Could you pull over?" This is a great exercise for character development and creativity.

> **Hint:** Players should come into the car with believable characters and try to be someone very different from the previous character. It is important to "give and take", instead of everyone talking at the same time and competing for focus. Make sure everyone contributes to the conversation before a new hitchhiker is picked up.

84   LAST LINE/FIRST LINE

Medium

Description: Players will have short conversations that begin with the words that ended another conversation. Two players have a conversation and at the end of three or four lines the facilitator says "Freeze." Two new players take their places and one of them starts a *new* and different conversation that begins with the last line of the previous conversation. In other words, the last line of one conversation becomes the first line of another conversation. The players should attempt to make the conversations as different from each other as possible.

For example:

Player A:	"Let's go get a hot dog."
Player B:	"Yeah, that would be great."
Player A:	"Great, I'll drive."
Facilitator:	"Freeze"
Player C:	"Great, I'll drive."
Player D:	"You might want to use your three wood."

Hint: Players should say the repeated line with a different voice or a new emotion to help take the conversation in a new direction. This exercise works best when it is acted out in short scenes.

85   I DIDN'T GO TO THE STORE

Medium

Description: Players will play a variation of the classic kids' game in which they say, "I went to the store and I bought a _____" and fill in the blank with items in alphabetical order. However, in this variation, players can do anything other than buy, and they can do it anywhere other than at the store.

For example: The first player says "I walked in a forest and saw an acorn." The next player says, "I walked in the forest and saw an acorn and a branch," and so on through the alphabet. When a player forgets an item, she can be eliminated, the other players can help her, or the game can start over. Some suggestions for different phrases are, "I went to Japan and saw a _____", "I looked inside an engine and found a _____", "I became a chemist and understood _____", "I went to a fine restaurant and tasted _____", or "I went to the moon and saw _____."

> **Hint:** Modify the phrase to something appropriate for your group. There are thousands of possibilities.

Variations:

1. The items are *not* chosen in alphabetical order. Each player can add a word beginning with any letter he chooses. This makes it easier to add a word, but more difficult to recall the order of the words that went before.

2. Items are required to be a specified number of words (two-word or three-word answers).

86   LIVING MACHINES

Medium

Description: The players will become the parts of an imaginary machine. The first player starts by entering the stage area and performing a repetitive motion with a noise. The other players enter one at a time and add a repetitive motion and noise to the machine. The players should be physically connected to each other in some way and should be in varied positions and heights (high, low, sideways, etc.). Two players can work together to become a sub-part of the whole (two players hold hands and one squats down as the other rises up).

Hint: Players should not start any movement that is too challenging because they will be doing it for a while.

Variations:
1. The facilitator can speed up the machine, slow it down, freeze it, run it backwards, have a part break, etc.
2. The players can become a specific machine such as sewing machine, or a car engine.
3. Specific machines can be made about topics such as the circulatory system or the economy.

87   STEREOTYPES

Medium

Description: Players will interact with each other based on given stereotypes. The facilitator makes a list of stereotypes and writes them on small, sticky labels. Examples of school stereotypes are jocks, A-students, cheerleaders, F-students, and most popular. The facilitator places these labels on the foreheads of players while ensuring the players do not see their assigned stereotypes. Then the players walk around the room for about ten minutes talking to others and treating them as though they were the stereotype on their forehead. The dialog and treatment should not be too obvious and players should not explicitly say what other players' stereotypes are. The stereotypes can be something appropriate for your group.

Discussion: Ask ❏ What was your stereotype? ❏ How did you come to that conclusion?

88   INVENTORY STORY

Medium

Description: A player will tell a story that includes all of the items on a list. The group generates a list of 10 to 15 unrelated nouns (people, places, or things). One or more players then tell a story that incorporates all of the items in the list. Words can influence the story subtly as in GRAB BAG on page 132.

Variation: Use this as a creative writing exercise with individuals or partners writing short stories that incorporate all of the items. Read the stories to the group to demonstrate how the same list of items can lead to stories that go in many different directions.

Discussion: This exercise demonstrates how the same starting point can lead to an unlimited number of possibilities. Ask ❑ How can you apply this idea to your own life?

89	TUG OF AIR

Medium

Description: The group will play a game of tug of war with an imaginary rope. Two people begin a game of tug of war, each pulling on one end of an imaginary rope. Gradually, players are added to both sides of the rope. The players need to act convincingly and remember that both sides cannot win, the rope is not elastic and it has a consistent width.

Discussion: Ask ❑ Did the rope look real? ❑ Why or why not?

90   TO MOVE, OR NOT TO MOVE

Medium

Description: Players will coordinate their efforts so that only one player is moving at a time. With the group standing in a circle, a designated player initiates any repetitive movement (raising one knee, lifting both elbows), while all the other players remain still. Every three to five seconds, any of the other players can initiate a different movement. At that time, the first player must stop his movement. The new mover must in turn stop her movement when another player initiates a new motion. Each player in the group must be aware of everyone else. The rotation should be random rather than a progression around the circle.

> **Hint:** This exercise is good for increasing awareness of one's surroundings.

Variation: At all times, exactly two players are moving. The number of movers can be increased up to the group size minus one.

Discussion: Ask ❑ Who went first? ❑ Who went last?

Our spontaneous action is always the best. You cannot, with your best deliberation and heed, come so close to any question as your spontaneous glance shall bring you.
Ralph Waldo Emerson

91	TWO ON ONE

Medium

Description: One player will simultaneously have two conversations with two other players. Three players sit side-by-side. The middle player carries on two different conversations with the other players. The two flanking players should not be distracted by the other conversation and should keep the pace as if it were a one-on-one conversation. The middle player should focus on being active in both conversations and turn her head from side to side as she speaks with each player.

> **Hint:** This is a challenging task that demonstrates how difficult it is to talk and listen at the same time.

92	RAP CIRCLE

Medium

Description: Players will create a rap song as a group. In a circle with an odd number of people, the players use their mouth, hands and feet to start a background beat for their rap song. One player delivers a line of rap music, and the next player in the circle adds a line that rhymes with the first. Then, the next player in the rotation delivers a line and the pattern continues. The players should try to keep the lengths of the lines consistent (like a poem). Whenever players are not singing, they should provide backup rhythm and sounds.

Variation: This can be done with two players with the pattern of delivering lines that is used in RHYME LINES on page 93.

93   WHAT IS IT?

Medium

Description: Players will use objects in mini-scenes. The facilitator gathers a bunch of different objects. The players stand around a table with their backs turned to the table. The facilitator places an object on the table and tells the players to turn around. The players then must use the object in a mini-scene, but it cannot be used in the way it was intended or be called by its real name. Not all players need to be in each mini-scene, and some mini-scenes will only have one player and be very short. Each item should be used several times before being replaced with a new item.

For example: The facilitator places a cellular phone on the table. When the players turn to look at the table, a player might grab the phone, hold it close to his heart and say, "My life is so much better now that I have this pacemaker."

94   LIMITED LINES

Hard

Description: The players will have a conversation in which the dialogue of all but one player is limited to written lines in books. Two or three players each grab a different book. A play works best, but a novel or even a textbook can be challenging and fun. The only lines these players can say are lines read from their books. Another player (without a book) is free to say anything and should say lines that tie the conversation together. Players with books should scan their books and quickly choose an appropriate line as the conversation develops. One of the players with a book should begin the conversation. It can be challenging and fun for the player without a book to justify the others' lines and to keep the continuity of the conversation going.

For example: Player A (with a book) might read a line that says, "Henry always gets the first pick." Player B (unlimited) might respond, "Well, that's because he's older. Now eat the tuna sandwich." Player A searches and finds, "Mrs. Smith certainly makes the best of it," to which Player B responds, "That's true. There was no mayonnaise left and these sandwiches are great!"

What you can't get out of, get into wholeheartedly.
Mignon McLaughlin

95   FREEZE ME OR PLEASE ME

Hard

Description: Players will begin mini-scenes based on the body position of players in the previous mini-scene. Based on a suggestion from the group, two people start a mini-scene with a lot of movement. After a few exchanges of dialogue, a player who is not in the scene shouts "Freeze." The players must immediately freeze in their current positions. The player who shouted "Freeze" replaces one of the players and assumes that player's exact position. The replacement player then initiates an entirely new scene starting in that position. This scene continues until another player says "Freeze" and replaces a player.

> **Hint:** It is important that players change positions often during the scene and make large movements so that the scenes do not begin from the same or similar positions.

Variation: After the new player assumes the position of the tagged-out player, the group suggests a new environment on which to base the next scene (at the beach, in a cave, etc.).

You will do foolish things, but do them with enthusiasm.
Colette

96   FREEZE-DOUBLE BLIND

Hard

Description: Players who have not been watching will begin mini-scenes based on the body positions of players in the previous mini-scene. Groups of players line up on both sides of the stage area with their backs turned to the two players on stage. A person not in the scene poses the two players on the stage as if they were mannequins. When the facilitator says "Start," the two players create a quick scene that somehow justifies their initial body position. They continue the mini-scene with exchanges of dialogue and accompanying movements until the facilitator says "Freeze" (after one or two exchanges), at which time they freeze in a new position. The two players who are at the front of the lines turn to see the two frozen players and quickly replace them in their exact frozen positions. When the facilitator says "Start," these two new players have to start an entirely new scene. Either player can initiate the first line of dialogue. The responding person should immediately accept the first line and say a line that adds to the scene. When the facilitator again says "Freeze" (after ten seconds or so), the next players in line jump out, replace the players and begin a new scene.

> **Hint:** It is important that the players assume the exact position of the tapped-out players. They should change positions often and make large movements so that the scenes do not all begin from similar positions.

Variation: Same as above except that all players are allowed to watch each scene.

97   INTRODUCE THE SPEAKER

Hard

Description: Players will give a short speech in a character assigned to them by the facilitator. The facilitator introduces a speaker, describing a few fictional things about him such as his background, hobbies, or interesting characteristics. The speaker does not know it is he who is being described and he who will give a speech until the end of the introduction when the facilitator looks at and points to him.

For example: The facilitator might say "As you all know, this next person has had a tough year. You may recognize him as the manager of the football team. His dad left his family earlier this year. He's shy, but tonight he has something powerful to share. Please welcome Zach." For the first time, Zach realizes it is he who is being introduced. Zach must come up to the front of the group and give a speech with the characteristics endowed to him by the facilitator.

The introduction can also be more playful. The facilitator could say something like, "She is a very rapid speaker", "He doesn't use words that start with 's'", "His mood vacillates between angry and ecstatic", etc. After a one-minute speech, the facilitator introduces another speaker. The name used does not have to be the speaker's real name.

> **Hint:** Begin with simple introductions.

Variation: A different person fills the introducer role each time a new speaker is introduced.

98 INTRODUCE THE INTRODUCER

Hard

Description: Players will give introductions for people while playing characters that were assigned to them. This exercise is like INTRODUCE THE SPEAKER, except the person who has just been introduced takes on her endowed characteristics and, instead of giving a speech, she introduces the next person in her assigned character. No speeches are given, just introductions. This string of introductions continues until everyone has been introduced and has introduced someone else.

99	TWO LINE SCENE

Hard

Description: Two players will establish a *who, what,* and *where* in two lines of dialogue (see page 154 for a discussion of *who, what* and *where*). One player initiates the first line, and the second player responds with another line. It is the players' goal that at the end of this short inter-action, *who* they are, *what* they are doing, and *where* they are will be clear. Players should use actions in addition to speaking to help define the who, what, and where, and shouldn't rush to speak.

For example: Player A begins by pushing a shopping cart and placing cans into her cart (miming), and says, "Three-ninety nine, that's outrageous for a can of tuna." The second player immediately adds to the role-play by stocking the shelves and saying, "Yeah, that Japanese boycott is sure driving the price up." The players must stop after the two lines, at which time the observers tell the *who, what,* and *where*. In this case, the *who* was a customer and stock clerk. The *where* was a grocery store. The *what* was shopping and reacting to the high tuna price. The players should rotate through the roles of initiator, responder, and observer.

> **Hint:** Players should avoid asking questions and put as much information as possible into each line. Actions help to define the *where*. Good character work defines the *who*. The *what* is usually the easiest to figure out.

Variations:

1. One player is the initiator who comes up with different first lines for all of the other players. There are still only two players and two lines in each scene, but one player plays the role of the person who says a different first line for each scene. The other players stand in a line and rotate through.

2. One initiator says the same first line for each of the other players who give different responses. There are still only two players and two lines in each scene, but one player delivers the same first line until each of them has responded with a unique second line.

100   JUSTIFICATION LINE

Hard

Description: Players will justify their actions in relation to dialogue that is not related to their movements. Two players begin with their backs turned to each other. Player A mimes some physical action, such as pulling on a rope or putting items in a box. Player B delivers a line of dialogue without seeing Player A's actions. Player A must then say something that justifies the action within the context of what Player B said. That is the end of that round and the speaker (Player B) becomes the mover while the next player in line becomes the speaker.

For example: Player A mimes something that looks like climbing a ladder. Player B (not seeing what Player A is doing) says, "My, it's getting foggy." Player A then might respond with, "Gee, I'm almost on the roof and it's not foggy up here."

Variation: If there are only two players, take turns as the mover and the speaker.

The thing about performance, even if it's only an illusion, is that it is a celebration of the fact that we do contain within ourselves infinite possibilities.

Daniel Day Lewis

101   GROUP POETRY

Hard

Description: Three or more people work together to compose a poem based on a suggestion. With three players, Player A says the first line, Player B the second line, Player C the third, and then back to Player A. The sequence continues until the poem is completed. The poems can be as long or short as the poets wish.

For example:

Player A:	High up in the trees was a bird who was big.
Player B:	He loved to sit up on the most highest twig.
Player C:	On one windy day, the big bird did proclaim
Player A:	I must leave this tree, or I will go insane.

This exercise can be played with up to ten people. If there is an even number of players, the pattern of delivering lines that is used in RHYME LINES on page 93 should be used.

> **Hint:** This can be tough to do at first, so it is okay to make mistakes and don't worry so much about rhyming; the important thing is to keep the poem going.

Anyone who takes himself too seriously always runs the risk of looking ridiculous; anyone who can consistently laugh at himself does not.

Václav Havel

CHAPTER 11

GAMES SPECIFICS

THESE 45 GAMES are some of the all-time improvisational classics. They allow people of all ages and backgrounds to become actors and perform like there's no tomorrow. Variations of many of them can be seen at local improv theaters or on the TV show *Whose Line is it, Anyway?* The games are short scenes that are made up on the spot (with no rehearsal), and they last around four to six minutes. Typically, three to four people work together following the rules of improv to develop a short scene that is shaped by some twist (the rules of each game) and based on a suggestion from the audience.

Improv games are great to do within small groups or to perform in front of an audience. They can be used to make a point during a business presentation, they are great for use during conferences or in classrooms, or they can be fun to play when you get together with your friends. You could even use these games to create your own improv entertainment night.

Like the exercises, the games have certain guidelines to follow. For example: A basic scene can be improvised just by following the rules of improv (commitment, acceptance, etc.), but in the game OPERA, the participants follow the same rules to create a scene with the twist that every word is sung like in an opera. The format of each game is specific, but within that structure the participants are free to create the content of the scene. These games become entertaining to perform and watch because of the restraints unique to each one.

Players should follow all the previously discussed rules of improv when performing these games (see Chapter 5), but the additional guidelines in this chapter should also be taken into account. Again, the emphasis should be on following the rules and staying within the structure rather than on trying to be funny and entertaining. It has been my experience that the most entertaining scenes happen when all of the players join together to follow the rules of improv instead of trying too hard to make the scene happen. It is following the rules and the players' commitment to their characters that help the scene to develop.

After you read the description for each game, have a small group do a quick demonstration to be sure that everyone understands the basic mechanics of the game. Then, divide into groups of four to perform each game based on a suggestion (see page 33). You can also have one small group of volunteers come in front of the whole group and per-form the game. Get a new suggestion each time the game is played.

BASIC FLOW OF A GAME

❏ Three or four people are brought in front of the audi-ence or selected from each small group.

❏ The facilitator explains the format of the game to the players and ensures the players and audience under-stand.

❏ A suggestion is solicited from the audience (Appendix C) upon which the players base the scene.

❏ The facilitator declares a clear start for the actors and the audience by loudly saying "Begin."

❏ The scene goes on for four to six minutes.

❏ Everyone has fun.

❏ The audience roars with applause.

It is rare that all of the players start a scene together. Usually, one player (or sometimes two) starts a scene, which goes on for 15 to 20 seconds before the next player comes in. The facilitator can choose the player(s) who will begin the scene. For beginners, it's okay if one player says a few words off stage to the other player(s) to set up the scene before it begins. For example: "We're in a grocery store, and I'm your mother." Also, scenes are more entertaining when characters move in and out of the stage area.

ADVANCED IMPROVISATION CONCEPTS

Before beginning the games, the facilitator should discuss miming and establishing the *who, what* and *where* of a scene. The *who, what* and *where* of a scene are developed through miming and dialogue, and it is the *who, what* and *where* that give a scene direction.

Miming: In general, the more action a scene has, the better it will be. Players should have a specific location (the *where*) in mind when they start a scene (a park, a kitchen, the moon, a lawyers office, etc.), and shouldn't feel rushed to start speaking. In one of the best scenes I've ever seen, two people spent almost a full minute pushing a car through the mud. It was entertaining because their miming (acting) was incredible. It really looked like they were pushing a car.

Spending time interacting with the environment makes the scene more interesting and leads to more obvious *what* possibilities. Scenes tend to be difficult and dull when the players just stand around talking. Carry something. Turn on a light. Make lunch. Light a fire. Open a can of pop and drink it with delight to show how hot and tired you are. Go through the files, pull one out, open it, gingerly remove a sheet of paper, and say "Ah, the Johnson file." All of these actions are easy when the players really *see* the items they are interacting with. The only props necessary are a couple of chairs or stools.

Miming should be the primary method of defining the *who, what*, and especially the *where* of a scene (discussed in greater detail below). There is a tendency for beginning improvisers to define their environment through words. For example: A player might say, "Hey, look at the waves. We're at the beach." It's much better to let the audience know where you are by interacting with the environment. This can be done best by mentally putting yourself in the *where*, and seeing and feeling the things that are there. Put on some sunscreen. Lie back on your towel and enjoy the heat of the sun. Pick the sand out of the egg salad sandwiches in your picnic basket. The possibilities are endless and will come to you if you put yourself there. If you really *see* the

153

objects you are interacting with, your miming will be more precise. Do the exercises MIME A ROOM (page 130) and PASS THE OBJECT (page 73) to practice miming skills.

Who, What, and Where: Every improv game or scene should have a definite *who*, *what*, and *where*. The sooner these are established, the easier the scene is for the players. Ideally, they are established within the first two or three lines. It is the responsibility of all players to help create these essentials for each scene, primarily through miming, but also through dialogue. The exercise TWO LINE SCENE (page 148) is very helpful for learning to define scenes.

Who: Simply put, the characters are the *who* of a scene. This is not just the names and roles of the characters (Mr. Jones the manager, Tammy the welder), but the traits that distinguish one character from another. Is the character sassy, easy going, old, young, clumsy, particular, happy, or grouchy? These types of attributes should be shown through the actions and words of the characters. A simple way to take on a character is by using a different posture or voice. Another way is to take on the characteristics of a person you know. It is easier to do these games if you become the character and let him guide your impulses in the scene. This takes you out of your head and lets you respond as that character rather than as yourself. If the scene calls for a feeble baggage carrier, the player should be as real as possible in becoming that character.

It is also really important that the players assume the characters already know each other and that the scene is a snippet of the ongoing story of their lives. It's like a sit-com. Even the first show doesn't begin with the characters meeting each other. There is a pre-established *who*, *what* and *where*. If a brother and sister start a scene, the first line wouldn't be "Hello, I'm your brother Tommy." Rather, it could be "Mommy, Leon stole my Lego again." It's the difference between going to dinner with an old friend versus going to dinner with a blind date. Avoid the blind date type of dialogue.

Where: It is very important that the players create the *where* for each scene (in a park, in a canoe on a river, at a bowling alley, etc.). The *where* is best defined through miming—actually interacting with imaginary items in the environment. The items are imaginary in that they are not really there, but the items should seem real to the players. With all the players paying close attention to the *where*, they can co-create the environment. For example: When someone opens an imaginary door into a restaurant, if the next player enters the scene through that door, the door and its handle should be in the same position on stage. If you're heading on a road trip, you might say "Let's go," and then walk to the car, open the door and get in, but how often do you say "Let's get into the car now" or "Here's the car"?

What: The *what* of a scene often flows naturally from well established *who* and *where*. Usually it is a normal occurrence: some conflict, a challenge to overcome, etc. Like in a movie or a play, there is something that happens, which can be as complicated as developing a formula to save the world from eminent annihilation, or it can be as mundane as a picnic without any forks. In any case, the *what* should be dealt with, and if the characters are committed within the structure of the game, they won't need a lot of *what*. Some beginners add too much *what*. For example: If a character is playing pinball, the *what* could be as simple as the ball getting stuck. The machine doesn't have to blow up or become a man-eating pinball monster or something crazy like that.

SCENE DEVELOPMENT

Scene development begins with establishing the *who, what*, and *where* of a scene and through following the rules of improv. The most important rules for scene development are commitment, acceptance, being specific, showing rather than telling, and not thinking. If players are 100% committed to their characters, they will react to whatever happens the way their character would react, and accepting whatever comes up as the reality of the scene is vital for moving the scene along. When players provide a lot of specifics, it gives the scene depth and direction, and scenes become more interesting when they involve action and visible emotions rather than a bunch of dialogue. Finally, players should go with their first reaction rather than thinking too much.

The audience suggestion gives the players an idea of where to start (see page 33), but it doesn't have to start in an obvious way. For example: If the suggestion is "the bank," the scene could start in a bank, while driving to the bank, one player could be a banker, characters could be doing something on the street in front of a bank, and so on. The suggestion just gives the players some idea of where to start.

If the request to solicit a suggestion is "Tell me a goal that someone has," the response might be "To climb Mount Everest." In this case, the scene could include everything it takes to climb Everest: a plane ride to Katmandu, the bus ride and hike to base camp, and the attempt to climb to the summit. A completely different direction would be imagining that a hill at the playground is Everest and the players are a colony of ants climbing it. The suggestion helps give the scene some direction by narrowing the focus.

Once the players on stage know the *who* of a scene (their characters are strong and the relationship between them is understood), a solid *where*, (in a car, outside at the park, at the office), and a clear *what* (the context of the scene, the conflict to overcome, what's going on), then the scene will take a direction of it's own. By following the rules of improv, scenes tend to go where they go, yet they go there as if that was the only possible choice. For example: If the suggestion for a scene is accounting, one player might start out by punching away at the calculator and becoming exasperated. The other player might carry in a load of papers (miming), and say, "Honey, three more hours and it will be midnight. Our taxes MUST be in on time." Right there we have a pretty clear idea of *who* they are (must be married because one said "honey," and they are doing their taxes together), *where* (some kind of office), and *what* (doing taxes). The relationship could be further defined if the second player said, in an impatient and frustrated way, "We could have used Uncle Phil. He was only going to charge $200." That would also add to the *what* by establishing a bit of a conflict between them. If the two players are committed to their characters and they continue to react and make choices the way their characters would, the scene could go on for hours.

In many of the games, especially where the same territory is covered more than once (FORWARD/REVERSE, REPLAY), it's best to start in the middle of some action. For example: If the suggestion is "picnic," instead of starting in the kitchen making sandwiches and then driving to the park, unloading, etc., the scene could start as dad is slicing the watermelon while Billy is roasting his hotdog over the fire. If the scene starts in the middle of the action, the *what* will come up sooner.

ENDOWMENTS AND INFLUENCES

Quite a few of the games call for performing a scene with different styles or influences, or assigning players various specific endowments. The range of types of endowments or influences is virtually unlimited. The box below includes a list of possibilities.

> Emotions, movie styles, famous characters, personality traits, a country, a state in the US, an age group, a magazine style, a genre of literature, a profession, a type of music, a decade in the last 100 years, or an animal.

An endowment or influence should never cause players to completely change the story line or deny something that has already happened. The influence should be more subtle. For example: If the endowment is a sports magazine, the topic shouldn't suddenly change to sports, but the characters might talk about training hard for the non-sports task they are doing or how their statistics have really improved this year. If a scene is at a car wash and the influence changes to western movie, the car wouldn't suddenly turn into a covered wagon, but the players might have western accents, say words like "pardner," and one character might talk like John Wayne. If the influence is "the 20s," things might be going really great and then all of a sudden go terribly, instead of the players suddenly throwing a stock market crash into the story line. If the endowment is a music style, the players could sing their lines in that style.

ENDING A SCENE

The facilitator should end the scenes. Knowing when and how to end a scene is not an exact science, and it is something that improves with practice. Generally speaking, scenes should last about four to six minutes. After a few minutes, the facilitator should pay attention to the flow of the scene and watch for a natural ending. When the scene gets to a logical conclusion or climax, the facilitator should end the scene in some assertive way, like blowing a whistle or yelling a declaration such as "Way to go", "Holy cow", or "Wowy cabowy!"

SETTING THE STAGE

Ideally, the stage is a raised area of at least fifteen feet by ten feet. A raised stage is especially important if there is a large audience. For a small audience, it's fine to clear an area of the same size and place the chairs in a semicircle around the cleared area. Narrowing down a larger area helps to create focus, and the players should perform within the boundaries of the stage and toward the front of the stage.

COSTUMES

Various costume pieces can make scenes more fun, but they are not essential. Some beginners want to "hide" behind a costume, so it might not be best to use costumes in the beginning. If you do decide to use them, a trip to the local thrift store can provide a large selection of items at a low cost. Things such as an oversized sports coat, glasses frames, wigs, hats, shawls, and a housecoat are very versatile. Players should use only one or two pieces that help define their characters and avoid over-doing it. A simple hat can help define an old lady or a train conductor. Keep costumes behind the stage area or somewhere that is hidden from the audience.

THREE-QUARTER STANCE

When performing for an audience, all of the players should face the audience or be in what is called the three-quarter stance. When two characters are talking to each other, the front of their bodies should be facing the audience as much as possible, even when they are looking at each other. Players should never be sideways or have their backs toward the audience.

Having a group of people perform the games is great fun for both the performers and the audience. Within the games you can practice hundreds of characters, play with ideas, learn to role play, etc. The games allow you to really connect with your fellow players in a way you normally wouldn't. They can break down the hierarchical structure of relationships (boss-subordinate, parent-child, etc.). Every new scene is an opportunity to try something new and, more importantly, to push yourself and get out of your comfort zone. There are scenes that will become magical and take on a life of their own; it's like surfing the perfect wave with three of your buddies.

CHAPTER 12

IMPROV GAMES

THESE ARE THE all-time great improvisational games that you might see at an improvisational theater. They are based on a suggestion from the audience, and they normally work best with three or four people and last about five minutes. It is as fun to perform them as it is to watch them. The games are more presentation oriented than the exercises, but they also work well in small groups with no audience. Many can also be used to make a point in a creative way. Most people learn better when material is presented in a way that is funny, different, or entertaining.

The skills practiced in many of the exercises help prepare players for the games and provide them with an understanding of improv, so it is important to warm up with some exercises before going on to the games. Even professional improv actors warm up before a performance.

1   BACK TO THE BASICS

Easy

Description: This is the most basic of all improvisation games. Players improvise a scene based on a suggestion from the audience. Unlike all the other games, which have some specific limiting rules, this is pure improv. Get a suggestion, then improvise a scene with good *who, what,* and *where.* Follow the rules of improv and see what happens. This scene can last a couple minutes or it could go on all evening. Most of the other scenes yield themselves to comedy; this plain and simple scene might or might not. Many theatrical plays are created by strictly adhering to the rules of improv.

2   ARMS EXPERT

Easy

Description: Two players work together as one Expert (on a suggested topic) and answer questions from the audience. Player A's arms become the arms of Player B. Player A stands behind Player B and puts her arms beneath his armpits and out in front of Player B while Player B wraps his arms around the back of Player A to get them out of the way (see the illustration). The Expert then answers questions from the audience. Player A begins answering by moving her arms while Player B verbally answers the question by justifying the arm movements. The arm movements should be bold, specific and natural. The speaker should accept the arm movements and the arm mover should react to the words of the speaker, but for the most part, the arms player leads the speaker by initiating movements.

For example: If the question from the audience is, "How do you plant a flower?" Player A might start by holding a pot (miming) in her hands. However, Player B may interpret the gesture as a posthole digger and respond with, "So grab your posthole digger, and start...." Player A should now have arm movements that support the new direction. This game works best if an extra large T-shirt is used to cover both players, and it's more comfortable for the "arms" if an 18-inch hole is cut in the back for the "arms'" head to poke out.

> **Hint:** The arms person should do many different and precise arm movements when attempting to answer the question. Some ideas are to outline objects or shapes, point at something, play musical instruments or sporting activities, climb something, etc.

Variations:

1. Another twosome (arms and talker) acts as the interviewer (like a talk show host).

2. The players act out a scene where the Arms Expert plays a character.

3   THE PROFESSOR

Easy

Description: Three players become one expert (the Professor) and answer questions from the audience on a suggested topic. Each player says one word at a time in rotating order, like in TWO SIDED on page 80. A fourth player acts as the host and somehow makes sense of the sometimes nonsensical answer of the Professor. The host can take on a game show host personality or any other interesting character. The host solicits each question from the audience, repeats the question loudly, and makes a comment that justifies the answer of the Professor after each answer is given. The three players becoming one should face the audience, enunciate, and speak loudly. They should try to speak as fast as they would if only one person were talking and try to the best of their ability to give an answer to the question. If they take on a certain character, they should all try to match each other so they sound and act as one.

Hint: Players should answer the questions by saying the first word that comes into their minds without hesitation. When players try to insert a word to be funny, it seldom works. This game will become entertaining just by sticking to the rules!

4   TWO FOR ONE

Easy

Description: One player is a normal character and two others will speak and act as if they are one person. Throughout the scene the players acting as one should alternate words when they speak (as in TWO SIDED on page 80). They should lock arms and carry out movements as though they are one character where the left arm of one player and the right arm of the other player work together. Because the two players are alternating their words, their dialogue may not always make complete sense, but the normal player should accept what they say, and try to fit it into the natural flow of the scene.

Hint: Players A and B should refer to their character as "I" and not "we".

5   FOREIGN MOVIE

Easy

Description: On the stage, two players perform a scene in Gibberish (see **GIBBERISH LESSONS** on page 95) while two off-stage players translate the dialogue in the scene. For example: Player A says, "Ya bosta, bla sto wooz mo." The off-stage interpreter, Player B might say, "Hey Micah, hand me the carrots, please." Then on-stage Player C says, "Shu bla reg mo steeg blan fa," and off-stage Player D might say, "Sure, here you go Jenny." The players on stage need to wait until they hear the translation before they reply to each other. The on-stage players should use a lot of action and specific movements to give the interpreters direction for scene. They should vary the lengths of dialog with some short, some long, and some one-word exchanges. When speaking Gibberish, allow the character to express as he/she would with emotion, intonations, etc. to support the character. Sometimes the interpreter may, if they like, respond with something other than the obvious at which time the on-stage players need to totally accept it as if they were their words.

> **Hint:** The Gibberish speaking players should really try to communicate with each other by showing emotions and interacting with the environment.

Variations:
1. The translators blindly translate the scene while facing away from the stage so they can't see the actions.
2. One of the off-stage interpreters comes into the scene and speaks Gibberish for their lines while continuing to interpret the other player's lines. This can be confusing but fun.

6   FOREIGN INTERPRETER

Easy

Description: One player who is the "expert" on a suggested topic speaks only in Gibberish while another player is the "interpreter" who can speak in both English and Gibberish. The interpreter solicits questions from the audience and translates those questions into Gibberish for the expert to answer. The expert answers the question in Gibberish, using strong facial expressions and gestures. The translator then translates the response into English for the audience, and so on. The translator should justify the "expert's" expressions and gestures in the translation.

> **Hint:** A short translation for a long line of Gibberish, or vice versa can be fun. So can an argument between the expert and the translator.

Variation: A player is a poet and recites a poem in Gibberish, and a translator interprets it. In order to help the translator, the poet should use gestures and put a lot of feeling into what he is saying. The poet should pause every couple of lines to allow for translation.

7 AUDIENCE SOUND EFFECTS

Easy

Description: One player makes up a story in front of the audience (see **WRITE ON** on page 177), and the audience provides sound effects where appropriate.

For example: If the story teller says, "The old man slammed the door," the audience members make an appropriate sound. The storyteller should be very descriptive while telling the story and should include a lot of action.

> **Hint:** Stress the importance of the story containing a lot of activity.

Variations:

1. Instead of one person telling a story, multiple players act out a scene and the audience provides appropriate sound effects.

2. This is like Variation 1, except an off-stage player or member of the audience makes random sound-effects now and then, and the actors then have to justify them within the scene.

| 8 | NEWSCAST |

Easy

Description: A suggestion of something minor that happened to someone recently is turned into a big newscast story. Sitting on a stool, the main anchorperson delivers a little of the everyday news before breaking into the "big story" (the suggestion solicited from the audience). She might say, "This just in. Sources tell us that a Janelle Johnson from Calabash, Iowa got a hair cut just a short while ago." The newscast might break away to a live on-location reporter who says, "That's right Jean. We're here live at Doug's Barber Shop...." The newscast might also include a brief interview with an authority on haircutting who owns haircutting schools across the country, which could be followed by a live, on-location report from Janelle's mother. "She never had a haircut like this...." The main anchorperson's job is to bring continuity to the newscast and tie up any loose ends. While the main anchor stays the same, the other players must "jump in" as needed.

Variations:
1. The news report is done in the style of a specific TV show such as *48 Hours, Entertainment Tonight,* or *Cops.*
2. An infomercial or commercial is developed based on a suggestion for a made-up product.

It is the child in man that is the source of his uniqueness and creativeness, and the playground is the optimal milieu for the unfolding of his capacities and talents.
Eric Hoffer

9	SLIDE SHOW

Easy

Description: Two or three players become the photo slides, and one or two players narrate the slide show based on a suggestion. The players who are the slides stand on stage with their backs turned to the audience. The narrator(s) sit to the side of the stage, facing the audience in a position where they can see the slides. There are two ways to call up slides. One way is for the narrator to set up the slide by saying something like, "In the next slide, you'll see Martha and Pete demonstrating the new technique in ironing men's wear." The posers should then turn around and quickly take that pose. The second way is for the posers to quickly pose however they want when a narrator says, "Let's see the next slide." The narrator(s) are then left to justify the pose by saying something like, "Notice the way Martha is expertly using the hard-fold technique to put a triple crease in Bob's pants." The posers turn their backs briefly in between slides.

Hint: The narrators can zoom in on a slide, have upside-down, stuck, or out-of-focus slides, or ask "How did that slide get in there?"

10   CROWD CONTROL

Easy

Description: The audience will determine which direction a scene will go. Two players start a scene. About every 20 seconds, the facilitator shouts "Freeze" at which time the two players on stage must freeze. Then the facilitator asks the audience, "And then what happens?" Individuals in the audience shout out several new directions for the scene. The facilitator takes one of the suggestions, repeats it out loud, and the players must then take the scene in this new direction.

Variation: The facilitator asks more specific questions such as, "Where do they go now", "Who's coming over", or changes something. For example: A player on stage says "Pass the soup," then the facilitator says "Freeze. It's not soup; it's…" Someone from the audience says "nail polish." "Nail polish it is. Players continue."

11   YOUR DAY YOUR WAY

Medium

Description: Players reenact and embellish an audience member's day. The facilitator asks someone in the audience to give a somewhat detailed explanation of an eventful day he has recently experienced. Then the players reenact that day with some embellishments.

Variations:
1. The day can be reenacted in a specific style such as an opera, a Shakespearean play, or a musical comedy.
2. The reenactment can begin before the eventful day or where the audience member's description of the eventful day ended.

12   CONDUCTED STORY

Medium

Description: A group of players jointly participate in telling a story. Three to six players stand close together facing the audience while the facilitator kneels down facing the players and controls who is telling the story by pointing to one of them. When, the facilitator moves his hand away from the person he was pointing to, that player must stop speaking, even if it is in the middle of a sentence or a word. At the same time, the facilitator randomly points to another player who must continue the story exactly where it left off, mid-sentence or mid-word. It is important to maintain the flow of the story. The facilitator can point to a player for anywhere between 2 and 10 seconds.

Variation: Each player tells their part of the story with a different influence. They can get endowments such as emotions, movie styles, ages, magazine styles, a particular state or country (see page 157 for a discussion on endowments and influences). It is important that the story make sense even though it is being told from different points of view. Players should focus on moving the story forward, not contradicting what has happened and just flavoring the story with their endowment.

13   NO LAUGHS

Medium

Description: Players perform a serious scene while another player comes in and out of the scene with outrageous characters attempting to make the other players laugh. The serious players should try not to be influenced by the antics of the clowning player. It is very important that the scene make sense in spite of the outrageous characters, which could include a rambunctious dog or a doting aunt.

Variation: One player is serious while the other players are various wacky characters.

14   END

Medium

Description: The audience determines how a scene will end. The facilitator solicits a specific ending for a scene from the audience. It can be a physical position (one player lying on the ground and the other standing on a chair pointing at him), a line of dialogue ("And that's why there aren't any more couches in Dover"), or anything else the audience can think of. Then the players create a four or five minute scene that ends in the suggested way.

> *Man is least himself when he talks in his own person. Give him a mask, and he will tell you the truth.*
>
> Oscar Wilde

15 DUBBING

Medium

Description: In this game, two off-stage players speak the words for two on-stage players who are moving their mouths and bodies as if the words were their own. It is important that the off-stage players speak slowly and deliberately while the on-stage players lip sync as best as they can with exaggerated mouth movements. The off-stage players should use distinctively different voices from each other. The on-stage players should be active and use their actions both to justify what is being said and to move the scene along.

Hint: Because the on-stage players do not do any speaking, this is a good game to play with people who are reluctant to talk or are worried about what to say.

Variations:

1. BLIND DUBBING: The off-stage players (who are speaking) face away from the stage and speak without watching what is happening in the scene.

2. LOCO DUBBING: The off-stage players enter the scene as new characters and speak for themselves while they continue to speak for the on-stage players. They should tilt their head down and use a different voice while speaking for the other player.

3. SOLO DUBBING: One off-stage player speaks for all on-stage players using distinctively different voices.

4. CROSS DUBBING: Two on-stage players speak for each other while attempting to lip sync the words being spoken for them. There are no off-stage players involved in this variation.

  CROSSROADS

Medium

Description: Two or three players start a scene, and every so often, when the players come to a major decision point or crossroad, an off-stage player shouts "Freeze" and offers the audience two contrasting scenarios for what happens next. The audience chooses one of the two paths, and then the on-stage players must continue the scene in the chosen direction.

For example: The mom says "Boy, it sure does stink in here." The off-stage player shouts "Freeze" and asks the audience to choose between "call in the Mighty Maids" or "immediate evacuation." The scene continues from there in the new direction.

17	SPELLING MACHINE

Medium

Description: One player acts as the announcer and asks the audience for a made-up word, and then two or three players (the Spelling Machine) stand side-by-side facing the audience and attempt to spell the made-up word. They act as one person, each player saying one letter at a time (like in THE PROFESSOR on page 162) followed by all Spelling Machine players emphatically saying the word together. Then they use that made-up word in a sentence (with each player saying one word at a time). After they finish, the announcer attempts to further define the fictitious word and comment on the sentence used. The players should try to make sense, but this game is fun even when they don't.

The following is an example of three players acting as one spelling machine with the suggested word Shatae:

Player A	Player B	Player C
S	H	A
T	A	E
	Shatae (all together)	
Drew	had	large
feet	so	he
went	to	the
store	to	purchase
a	shoe	that
resembled	a	shatae
	Shatae (all together again)	

Then the announcer says something like, "That's right! Shataes, ancient Egyptian party slippers, really make your feet look smaller."

Hint: It is important to let go of independent ideas, concentrate on working as a team, and to say the first word that comes to mind.

18   OLD-TIME RADIO

Medium

Description: Players perform an old-time radio show like radio actors did in the old days. Three or four players sit together in front of the audience and improvise an old-time radio program based on a suggestion for a made-up title. The story line is very important and should include action, but the players don't make actual movements; they just add sound effects. The characters should be dramatic like those in soap operas. One player can be in charge of sound effects like they had in the old days.

Hint: Try turning the lights out for a real radio feel. Accompaniment by an organ player adds fun and drama.

19   EMOTIONAL PARTY

Medium

Description: Each of the players solicits an emotion from the audience and then the players act out a scene with their assigned emotions. The emotions selected should be very different from each other. Like most other scenes, the scene is based on suggestions solicited from the audience.

20   ENTRANCES AND EXITS

Medium

Description: Players will enter and exit a scene when a specific word is said. Before beginning the scene, each player solicits a common word from the audience. The players then perform a scene, and anytime their assigned word is said in the scene, they must either enter or exit the stage area (depending on whether they are on or off the stage). The players must also justify within the scene why they are coming or going. An on-stage player may say his own word in the context of the scene if he desires to exit.

> **Hint:** For fun, assign someone a conjunction like "and", "or", "but", or "also". She will pop in and out of the scene very frequently.

21   FILM DIRECTOR

Medium

Description: Players will produce a movie while one player acts as the director. The facilitator gets a suggestion for a title of a movie that has never been made. Then one player acts as the director of the movie, and the others are the actors.

For example: The director might say, "Okay, we're starting with scene five where the knights have a picnic. And, action." The actors then improvise that scene. The director can direct the actors to do anything, such as changing the dialogue of a scene, reenacting a scene with more passion, or skipping segments of the movie.

22   WRITE ON

Medium

Description: One player sits facing the audience and dictates or writes a novel, and the other players periodically provide "live" excerpts from the novel. The writer can pretend to type at a computer or write by hand as she voices aloud what she is writing. The story goes back and forth between the novelist and the other players, with both contributing to and advancing the story. The players should add both dialogue and action to the story. The characters stand with their backs turned to the audience while they aren't acting, ready to take over any time the author pauses. When the author begins again, the characters turn their backs to the audience. It should be a give and take between the author and the characters in the novel with each episode lasting ten to fifteen seconds.

For example: The author might say "It was becoming treacherous out there on the sea. Captain George was showing signs of despair...." Right away, the characters turn around and the action starts as Captain Bob takes over at the helm of the boat.

> **Hint**: The novelist can stop and rewrite parts of the scene. The characters may do something, and the novelist could "erase" those lines and say "No, that doesn't work. 'He said goodbye as if it were his dying words...'"

Do it big, or stay in bed.
Larry Kelly

23	REPLAY

Medium

Description: Two or three players perform a short scene they will then reenact with different influences. After the players create a 30- to 60-second scene that is concise and includes a lot of action, the facilitator calls time and asks the audience for three different styles such as a type of movie, an emotion, or a music style (see page 157 for a discussion on endowments and influences). The players then replay the scene three times, once in each different style. It is important to keep the story line the same as it was originally performed; it should just be "bent" to fit the style.

For example: In the original scene the players drive to a lake, go swimming, and then have dinner. If the three styles are western movie, happiness, and jazz, the first replay might involve riding a stagecoach to a waterhole and then eating vittles at the chuck wagon. In the second replay, the players would express great happiness in all they do as they recreate the scene, and in the final replay, they might sing jazzy tunes as they drive, swim and eat. Other types of influences that can be used include magazines, ages, countries, states in the US, or any other influence that can be imagined.

24	SLOW MOTION

Medium

Description: In this game, two players perform a competitive event while two other players provide the play-by-play commentary. The facilitator gets a suggestion from the audience for a mundane task (dry cleaning, pickle making, tire changing). Two players then perform this task as a new Olympic event in slow motion and without speaking. Two other players sit nearby and act as commentators who make sense of the competitors' movements. Occasionally, the commentators can lead the players by saying something like, "John's opening the refrigerator and about to make the sandwich. He's only got 10 seconds left. Let's see what happens." The two players on stage should move very slowly and at the same speed as each other. They can either compete against each other or as a team.

> **Hint:** The competitors should really exaggerate their movements and facial expressions. It can be really funny when a mundane task is full of drama.

25   ENDOWMENTS EXCHANGE

Medium

Description: Players will take on the emotions or endowments of other players as they enter and exit a scene. Each player is assigned an endowment such as an movie style or personality trait (see page 157). The scene starts with one player. As each new player enters the scene, all players take on the assigned endowment of that player, and as each player leaves (in reverse order), they revert back to the previous endowment.

26   MOVIE STYLES

Hard

Description: Players will periodically change styles while creating a scene based on a suggestion. The facilitator solicits a list of about ten types of movies (western, silent, drama, action, kung fu, etc.) from the audience. The players start a basic scene and let it run about 30 seconds before the facilitator shouts out one of the movie styles. The on-stage players then continue the scene as if it is that type of movie. The facilitator randomly calls out the different styles every 20 to 30 seconds. Changing too fast can create a disjointed scene. Review the endowments and influences section on page 157 to understand how the movie styles should subtly influence the scene.

> **Hint:** Players should focus on maintaining the same basic story line when the style changes.

Variations:
1. Instead of types of movies, the scene is enacted with other influences such as different kinds of music or magazines, literary styles, countries, or animals. Remember, the influences should be subtle.
2. Different types of influences are combined, such as one music style, one country, and one animal.

Make visible what, without you, might perhaps never have been seen.

Robert Bresson

27	MOOD SWINGS

Hard

Description: Players create a scene full of mood swings. The facilitator solicits a list of about ten emotions from the audience, and then two players begin a normal scene. After about 20 seconds, the facilitator shouts out one of the emotions and both on-stage players take on that emotion and continue the original scene. The facilitator continues to call out emotions every 10 to 20 seconds starting with easy emotions (such as happy or sad) then moving on to more complex emotions (such as apathy and paranoia). Players should focus on keeping the scene moving in the same direction without contradicting the established reality. A new emotion does not mean a different scene and shouldn't cause the players to deny what has already happened in the scene.

> **Hint:** The timing of the facilitator is important. It is best to change right before an emotional reaction is expected. If the audience is expecting a reaction of anger, shout out "love."

Variation: Instead of one person calling out emotions, there are two off-stage callers, one assigned to each player. The off-stage callers should not call out the same emotions.

You probably wouldn't worry about what people think of you if you could know how seldom they do.

Olin Miller

28 FORWARD/REVERSE

Hard

Description: Players will perform a scene in which they periodically change from going forward in the scene to repeating parts of the scene in reverse. The players begin a scene, and after a couple exchanges of dialogue accompanied by actions, the facilitator (or an off-stage player) shouts "Reverse." At that time, the players must go backwards in the scene, reversing the order of their actions and statements, but not the words in each statement (their statements will still sound normal). When the facilitator says "Forward," the players move forward in the scene, repeating what they have already said and done and continuing onward. The facilitator periodically shouts out "Forward" or "Reverse" throughout the scene (about every two or three exchanges). Limiting the dialogue and including a lot of action helps players remember what was said earlier.

Hint: Keep the scene progressing forward by doing reverse for a short time and then a longer forward so that the scene goes in to new territory on most exchanges. Also, the caller should not go too long before calling "Reverse" because it becomes hard for the players to remember what has been said. Toward the end of the scene, the caller can let the players on stage attempt to back up to the beginning. It is even possible to allow the reverse to go beyond the beginning of the scene at which time the players must create the dialogue and actions that came before the point when the scene began.

Variation: The caller can say, "Fast forward" (players go in fast motion and talk as fast as they can), "Fast reverse", "Pause", "Forward in another language", etc.

29   EMOTIONAL BOUNDARIES

Hard

Description: Players perform a scene in which they change emotions as they move around the stage. The stage is divided into three zones (left, right and middle), and each zone is assigned a particular emotion. The players create a scene, and as they move about the stage they take on the emotion of the zone they are in. The three emotions should be simple and contrasting. Players should justify their movements between zones within the context of the scene.

Variation: This game can be played with other influences, such as types of movies or literature, professions, political parties, or ages (see page 157 for a review of endowments and influences).

30 THE THING HE SAID WASN'T WHAT HE REALLY MEANT, THIS IS WHAT HE REALLY MEANT GAME

Hard

Description: While players A and B act out a scene on stage, players C and D are off stage, voicing the on-stage player's thoughts. Each time one of the on-stage players speaks, the off-stage player states what the on-stage player is really thinking. The players on stage should accept what the off-stage voices are saying to be the reality of their thoughts and be subtly guided by them. For example: If an on-stage character said, "This cake is great," her off-stage voice might say, "Yuck, did he dump half a box of baking soda into the batter?" The on-stage player might then look like she is trying not to grimace and would eat much less enthusiastically.

184

31 SCENE IN VERSE

Hard

Description: Players perform a scene that rhymes. They are free to speak at will except that every two lines must rhyme with each other. Line one and two should rhyme with each other as should lines three and four, etc. If Player A has dialogue that consists of three lines, his first and second lines must rhyme, and then he can say a third line. Player B then says a line that rhymes with Player A's third line. For example: Player A says, "Oh my goodness, I'm out of eggs. I'll run to the store; I have fast legs. While I'm gone, you stir the soup." Player B replies, "Is that what it is? I thought it was slimy goop." It can be challenging to maintain a coherent scene.

Variations:
1. Each player can only speak one line before another player speaks a line.
2. The scene is based on a suggestion of a specific poetic or rhythmic style, such as Shakespeare, Robert Frost, or a limerick.

For God's sake give me the young man who has brains enough to make a fool of himself!

Robert Louis Stevenson

32   HESITATION

Hard

Description: Players perform a scene in which the audience supplies the next word whenever a player hesitates. Two or three players start a scene and hesitate periodically, by saying, "Um, um, um." At this time, someone from the audience shouts out a word that the player must use as his next word. The shouted word does not have to be a logical word for the scene; however, it needs to be grammatically correct.

For example: A player is in the kitchen opening the refrigerator door and says, "Oh boy, I am so hungry I am going to grab the um, um, um." An audience member shouts out "typewriter." The player must accept and say the word typewriter and continue the scene in a way that typewriter makes sense. His next sentence might be, "Mom! Someone ate the home row." Then the mom guiltily asks, "What do you mean?" to which he replies, "See! There's the L stuck in your teeth." The scene continues from there. The challenge is to deal with whatever comes up from the audience, not just once, but throughout the scene. The players must go with the first comprehensible word they hear from the audience, as long as it's clean.

> **Hint:** After each hesitation in the scene, the players should work with the new word and justify it before they hesitate again.

Variation: One player starts a motivational speech and hesitates as above. The audience then fills in the next word of her speech. "The three keys of success are planning, execution, and um, um…" "hamburger."

33   SHOULD HAVE SAID

Hard

Description: Players will have a conversation that the facilitator can make them change at any time. Several players have a conversation. Anytime during the conversation, the facilitator can interrupt the players by saying "should have said." At this time, the player who was interrupted must change the last line she said to something entirely different and the conversation should continue in that new direction. If the facilitator is still not satisfied with the new line, the facilitator can say "should have said," again. The player comes up with another new line that alters the course of the conversation.

Variations:
1. Actions are included along with the conversation.
2. When the facilitator says "should have said…" the audience fills in the blank.

34   SHAKESPEARE

Hard

Description: A scene is played as if it were a Shakespearean play. This game is straightforward, but it can be demanding. These plays usually involve betrayal, intrigue, or revenge. It is fun to see mundane situations acted out with the drama and conviction of Shakespeare's characters. The Big Gulp machine running empty at the local 7-Eleven could become a modern tragedy.

> **Hint:** It is helpful to use an English accent and the words associated with Shakespeare's writing such as hark, thy, upon, and goest.

35   SING A SONG

Hard

Description: One of the players (or a group of players) makes up a song about a topic solicited from the audience. It helps to have some musical accompaniment, but it is not necessary. It is important to have a good story line as well as to try to rhyme. One player can lead the song, and the others can be backup singers, or each player can make up a line in an orderly rotation.

> **Hint:** Slow music is easier than fast music, and it is helpful to have a refrain to come back to.

Variations:
1. The facilitator gets a suggestion for the style of music (rap, opera, country, folk, etc.).
2. Set it up as a music awards show with three different songs in three different musical styles based on the same suggestion.

188

36 MANNEQUIN

Hard

Description: Two or three players in a scene can speak but they cannot move their bodies by themselves; a designated "mover" performs that function for them. The mover moves the players by standing behind them and moving their various body parts as he sees fit (waves their hands, nods their heads, bends them over, etc.). The players being moved should not resist the movement, and their dialogue should jive with how their body is being moved. The mover has to really fly between the all the players to keep them moving.

Variation: This can be done with two actors and two movers.

37	OPERA

Hard

Description: Players perform an opera based on a suggestion. The entire scene is sung and should follow an improvised story line. Players should include a lot of action in the songs and act it out so they don't just stand and sing. It works best when one or two players have the focus while the other players provide backup singing. When one person has the focus, the others can back them up with simple "do whop" type singing or by repeating single words that the lead singer has sung. Players should vary the tempo and volume and sing with passion.

> **Hint:** Be sure to establish a clear who, what, and where, and keep in mind that operas often have a villain and a hero or heroin. It's fun when the singing and action builds up to a resolution with everyone singing.

38	FOREIGN OPERA

Hard

Description: One player is a narrator for an opera that the other players in the scene perform in Gibberish. Unlike FOREIGN MOVIE, the narrator does not need to translate every word or sentence as it happens. Occasionally, the narrator can speak over the songs in the opera by telling the audience what is happening or what will be happening next in the scene. Because the players do not have to worry about dialogue, they should sing with as much passion as possible. The other players in the scene can provide backup singing when they are not the main character(s) in the scene. It is very important to have a scene with lots of activity. It is fun to lead up to a crescendo at the end of the scene.

190

39   SIT, STAND, KNEEL

Hard

Description: This scene has three players and, at all times, one player is sitting, one player is standing, and one player is kneeling. All the movements should make sense within the scene. For example: A scene starts with a boy doing his homework on a computer (sitting). His father comes into the room and notices his son's report card on the floor (standing). Soon, the mother enters the room (standing). At that time, the father kneels down to pick up his son's report card (to satisfy the sit, stand, kneel requirement). He might then stand up and comment on the straight A's, at which time the mother might go to her knees weeping for joy. Very challenging! This game is extremely difficult, so it might be better to start with one of the easier variations below.

Variations:
1. All players sit but one. The other player can be doing anything.
2. All players stand but one.
3. One player is always walking.
4. Make up any other limiting condition.

You grow up the day you have your first real laugh at yourself.
Ethel Barrymore

40   SCRIPT SCENE

Hard

Description: Three players create a scene in which all of the dialogue of two players comes from written text (see LIMITED LINES on page 143). Plays work best, but a novel or textbook can be fun and challenging. The scene should be based on a suggestion, and should begin with one player with limited lines and the player who can speak freely. The player who can speak freely should make statements rather than asking questions. The script-reading players should participate in the scene as well as scanning their material for the next appropriate line to contribute. The non-reading player needs to stay on her toes to make sense of the scripted statements and move the scene along. The script readers should read an appropriate line as often as possible.

41   BROADWAY MUSICAL

Hard

Description: Players perform a scene like a musical. There is normal dialogue, but players frequently break into a song and dance routine. "Grease" and "The Sound of Music" are familiar examples. The songs should move the scene forward instead of rehashing what has already happened. Songs should not last long and should happen whenever there is a twist or conflict in the scene. The lead singer should be obvious while the other players provide background singing and dancing. This game is different from OPERA in that it has speaking parts as well as singing.

Variation: Someone plays a piano or other instrument, and whenever they start playing (at their discretion), the actors must break into song and dance. The musician can play any simple background music that they make up as they go along. This can be really fun, so don't be afraid to try it.

192

42   RADIO STATION DIAL

Hard

Description: Each player is a different radio station. The facilitator asks the audience for a different radio style for each station such as jazz, country western, classical, talk, or rock. In addition, the facilitator asks for a topic or attribute for each player that the players will mix with their radio styles. The topic could be an emotion, a type of food, a magazine, or a famous person. The players could end up with something like banana rap, angry opera, or Swedish country western. The players stand shoulder to shoulder and face the audience while the facilitator kneels in front of the group (like in CONDUCTED STORY on page 170). The facilitator points to one player at a time, which "tunes" the radio to that player's station. When the facilitator pulls her hand away and points to another player with her other hand, the first station is off and the radio is immediately switched to the new station.

> **Hint:** Players should remember to start in the middle of a song or conversation rather than always at the beginning, as if you were turning the dial in your car. Also, the timing of the pointing is important. The pointer should point to players for a few lines at first and then vary the length of time between stations.

Variation: Try it as a television dial with different types of television programs, such as a soap opera, news, talk show, late night entertainment, classic movie, or sports.

43	ACTIVATE

Hard

Description: Two players will get a third player to do an activity without using any intelligible words. The facilitator selects a volunteer and asks him to leave the room. While the volunteer is gone, the facilitator asks the group for an activity for the volunteer to do (playing cards, bowling, painting a house, etc.) and then has the group embellish the activity. The facilitator might say, "We'll get him to play cards; however, he's somewhere you wouldn't normally play cards. Where is he?" Someone might say, "On the moon," so the volunteer will be playing cards on the moon. The volunteer is then invited back to the room, and two players get the volunteer to perform the activity without first doing the activity themselves and without speaking intelligible English. They have to use Gibberish (see **GIBBERISH LESSONS** on page 95) to communicate and act out the scene with the volunteer. The scene should make sense and have a logical progression.

In this example, the knowing players might get the volunteer in a space ship, fly to the moon, land, get out and set up a card table. Next, one of them might pull some make-believe cards from his pocket, shuffle them, and hand them to the volunteer. Hopefully, the volunteer will initiate playing cards. When the volunteer looks as if he knows what he is doing, the facilitator asks the volunteer, "What are you doing?" and he should say, "I'm on the moon playing cards." The activities can be embellished even more as the players get comfortable with this game. For example: "On the moon playing cards on a toaster with Barney".

> **Hint:** Strong miming and a strong story really help the volunteer figure out what he is doing. Also, encourage the volunteer to be an active participant. If he is handed what looks like a basketball, he should do the next logical thing like bounce the ball or shoot the ball. The knowing players should steer the volunteer in the right direction.

I have yet to see any problem, however complicated, which, when you looked at it in the right way, did not become still more complicated.

Poul Anderson

44   POETRY

Hard

Description: Players each make up a poem. The facilitator asks the audience for a poetic style and a topic for each player, and then the players make up a poem in their given style on their chosen topic. Some examples of types of poetry include haiku, Edgar Allen Poe, or Dr. Seuss. The players should concentrate on moving the poem forward as well as making it rhyme.

Variation: This can also be done with each poet creating a poem on the same subject in different styles, or it can be done with poems on different subjects all in one style.

45   POETRY GROUP

Hard

Description: Players work together to make up a poem. Three to six players stand on stage and face the audience. The facilitator solicits from the audience a title for a poem that has never been written. One player starts the poem by reciting the first line. The next player recites a second line, and so on until the poem is complete. The players should focus on the poem making sense in addition to rhyming. It is also best to keep the length of the lines similar.

Variation: Pick a musical style and sing the poem as above.

CHAPTER 13

CLOSURE ACTIVITIES

It's always beneficial to have some kind of closure activity at the end of your session, even if it's only for a few minutes. The purpose of most of these exercises is to summarize what happened, what players learned, and how they can apply their learning to their life. These are facilitator-led exercises like the whole group exercises. Before the players leave, remind them that they can practice these exercises later with their friends or family, and thank everyone for their willingness to follow the rules and take a risk.

THE CLOSURE DOZEN

1: Only One Thing To Do

Directions: Ask the group to think about one thing they learned today that they will immediately incorporate into their lives. Divide the group into partners and ask them to share their answers with each other.

2: Last Stand

Directions: Have three or four players come up and tell or show what they learned today by singing it, performing it in the style of one of the games, saying it in a specified number of words, doing an infomercial, etc.

3: 30 Seconds of Life

Directions: Have two or three people come up one at a time and summarize what they learned today in 30 seconds. Ask for volunteers who normally wouldn't do something like this.

> **Hint:** You can ask for volunteers by saying something like, "There are three people in this room who wouldn't normally come up and share with the group. You're sitting there thinking to yourself, 'I normally wouldn't do this, but today, I'm going for it.' ... You know who you are."

Variation: Be more specific. For example: "Summarize the three key points to today's session," or "Tell us how this improv stuff can be applied to our jobs," or "What is the most important thing you learned about yourself today?"

4: Start, Stop, Continue

Directions: Ask the group to think about what they learned today and then to write down one thing they will start doing differently, one thing they will continue to do, and one thing they will stop doing. Ask them to share this information with a partner.

5: Trust Wave

Directions: Divide the group in half and have players stand shoulder to shoulder to form two parallel lines about four feet apart. Demonstrate by running through the double lines holding both hands up and giving high fives to both lines. Then, beginning at one end, have each player run through in the same way and rejoin the line at the other end. After everyone has gone through giving high fives, ask the people in the line to put their arms out in front of them and touch fingers with the person across from them. Then, one at a time, have the players run through the line as fast as they can while all other players raise their hands just before the running player passes by and then lower them after he has passed. It is as if the person is creating a wave as he runs. Repeat this process as many times as you want.

> **Hint:** It can be scary at first to run toward the players with their arms out. It gets easier each time so players should get faster. This exercise requires a great deal of trust that others will raise their arms in time. Really emphasize the need to pay close attention when standing in the line so that players do not hit the person running through.

Variation: Choose a self-revealing phrase for the players to complete and shout before they run through the line a second time. For example: "One thing I learned today is _____," "What I want you to know about me is _____," or "A goal of mine is _____."

6: The Last Laugh

Directions: Tell the group that on the count of three, everyone is going to laugh as big as they can—for no reason at all. This will last for at least 10 seconds, and everyone must make eye contact with at least three different people. This exercise can be really fun because some people will get really tickled by it and won't be able to stop laughing. This then becomes contagious and others continue laughing with them beyond the 10 seconds.

Variation: This exercise can be done in small groups with people lying on the floor in a circle, so that each person's head is on another person's stomach (feet pointing out). Instead of just laughing for 10 seconds, one person starts by saying a forceful "Ha." The next person says "Ha, ha," and so on until everyone has said one "ha" more than the person before them. This exercise causes the most uncontrollable laughter with the young and the young-at-heart.

7: Nothing Is Wrong

Directions: Have everyone sit down, close their eyes and relax. Tell them to visualize themselves walking down a path. Have them notice what they are wearing and feel the ground as they walk. Take your time; give them time to "see" and "feel" it. Ask them to notice the trees and hear the sounds of the birds. Then tell them that in the distance they see a bench in the middle of a meadow. When they reach the bench they sit down and feel the warmth of the sun. They just sit there... And they realize that absolutely nothing is wrong.... Nothing is wrong with anything.... Have them really feel it. Let them sit quietly for a minute or two and then say goodbye.

8: Spider Web

Directions: Have players stand or sit in a circle. The first player holds onto the end of a ball of yarn and tosses it across the circle to someone while saying something nice about her or commenting on something she did well. She catches it, holds onto the string, and tosses it to someone else while complementing that person. Each person should only get the yarn once until an intricate pattern is formed and everyone is connected.

> Hint: After everyone is connected, the leader can comment on how we are all connected together in friendship, community, or something appropriate for that group.

9: Compliment Circle

Directions: Have players sit in a circle. Someone begins by complimenting the person next to him. Then everyone else in the group compliments that person. She then complements the person next to her followed by everyone else in the group. This goes on until everyone in the group has been complimented. Each person being complimented must say "Thank you" and nothing else.

10: Harmonious Hands

Directions: Ask players to raise their right hand. Then ask them to lower their right hand and raise their left hand. After a couple of times, have the players hold hands. Say, "While holding hands with your neighbors, raise your right hand," (which will automatically raise the left hand of the person they are holding hands with). Then say "lower your right hand." Next have them raise their left hands and then lower their left hands. Repeat this process a couple of times. You will see people struggle and laugh. Then ask, "What has to happen to your left arm in order for your neighbor's right arm to go up?" They should relax and stop fighting it. When they are aware that they need to relax and not resist, repeat the commands.

Discussion: There should not be a struggle, but inevitably there will be one. Ask ❏ Why was there a struggle? ❏ Why did some people make it hard for others to raise and lower their hands? ❏ What do you need to be conscious of?

11: Here's To You

Directions: Say "I'd like to have everyone stand up and applaud each other around the room." You can demonstrate by walking around and randomly applauding individuals. This exercise can become very contagious if you let it go for a while, and it makes everyone feel good.

12: By the Book Closure

Directions: Ask what players learned today. After a few responses ask, "What did we learn about _____ (and fill in the blank with teamwork, communication, creativity, etc.)?" Then ask "How can we use what we learned and apply it toward _____ (and fill in the blank with learning, getting along, freedom, etc.)?"

CHAPTER 14

A LIFETIME OF SPONTANEITY

WHEN I THINK of spontaneity, I usually associate it with freedom. Some of the most fun and memorable times I've had have been random moments, usually in the company of good friends, that just happened. Think about the most enjoyable times in your life; I bet many of them were also some of the most unexpected and unplanned moments.

Improvising on their own is what kids do best. With a little practice, we can relearn how to improvise as adults. Whether it's making up songs at home, putting together random ingredients for dinner, telling stories in the car, starting your own business, or inventing new games, the following rules of improvisation will start you on your way. By committing 100%, accepting everything that comes up, following the rules, having no attachment to the outcome, and not allowing side talking, it will become easier to improvise and be spontaneous, and to get lost in the magic that can happen.

COMMITMENT

Watch kids play. They are 100% engaged in what they are doing. That's what we're after here. When you decide to paint, write, act or play, focus all of your attention on what you're doing. One time while I was on an airplane, I began talking to the distinguished man sitting next to me. We discussed his high-up job in Washington, DC, and then we started talking about how seriously we take ourselves as adults. He told me that he and his wife used to have fun, but that lately, with all the seriousness of their lives, they rarely do. As the conversation became more philosophical, I sneaked a little rubber booger out of my briefcase. I'd just received it as a birthday gift and had never tried it out in public, but I faked a sneeze (with 100% commitment), and when I removed my hands, there was a realistic looking three-inch dangler hanging from my nose. After the initial shock, my new friend really cracked up.

Thinking about my friend's self-admitted need to take himself less seriously, I went to the washroom and cleaned the plastic prop. When I came back to my seat I said, "If you put this in your nose and sit here for awhile, it will make my day. But if you put it in and walk all the way down the aisle and back with a straight face, you'll really make my week." After five minutes of some coercion on my part, he finally said "Give it to me; I'm walking." I followed a few paces behind as this grown man in a business suit (the boss of hundreds of people at the state department), walked down the aisle of the plane with a dangler hanging out of his nose and a totally straight face. Most people didn't look up, but those who did had some shocked faces, to say the least. By the time we landed in Denver he wanted to keep it. Seventy-nine cents at a gag gift shop, no problem. "My gift to you," I said. "Here's my card; let me know what happens."

A couple of days later he called and left me a message telling me about the fun he'd had on the next leg of his flight to DC, his wife's initial shock and how the two of them laughed hysterically. He called again about four months later to tell me about all the new and fun things he and his wife were doing—dance classes, random trips, whacky times—all because of a 79 cent piece of plastic and 100% commitment. So when you get the urge, go for it with 100%. Don't hold back.

ACCEPTANCE

Acceptance here means accepting everything exactly as it is and accepting whatever happens as it happens. The other day a song I like came over the speakers at a coffee shop so I asked my friend to dance. She immediately stood up, and we danced there in the crowded shop. We had a fabulous time. I offered; she accepted. Once when my son Charles was three, we went swimming at an athletic club. Afterwards, we were in the changing room with about 25 macho guys who had just finished their workouts. Charles, always in his own world, started singing the ABCs song. A big dude standing next to him looked down and chimed in with "H, I, J, K, L, M, N, O, P..." Soon everyone was singing and, for a few minutes, we were all like children and everything was okay. Acceptance means saying yes to whatever comes up. Great musical improvisers do this well, accepting and supporting each other as the music "happens." Try doing this in your everyday life.

NO ATTACHMENT TO OUTCOME

There is a big difference between following a recipe and winging it, painting from scratch versus painting by number, or having everything planned down to the minute for your vacation rather than going somewhere and allowing things to happen.

I recall the feeling of excitement I had back in my early twenties while hitchhiking across New Zealand. I never knew where I would sleep each night or where I was headed next. Some nights I ended up in a youth hostel, sometimes in a tent and occasionally families invited me into their homes. There was incredible freedom in not following a rigid schedule and trying to fit everything in. I had no expectations, so I experienced no disappointment.

When we allow ourselves to occasionally "experiment" with life (just create for the heck of it) without trying to accomplish, impress, prove or justify, we can experience a remarkable feeling. What happens happens, and whatever is is exactly right. I don't know about you, but my best pool shooting happens when I don't care about winning. In the same way, my best speeches happen when I'm not too worried about how they will turn out. The funniest and the most profound moments aren't planned. They happen because I and the people I am speaking to are just being present and totally focused on the moment.

Not too long ago, I met a friend at a coffee shop. Soon, out of the blue, a couple of our other friends walked in. We all happened to have time for lunch so we spontaneously walked across the street to a sushi restaurant. While we were waiting to order, the conversation turned to the topic of attachment and how we get so attached to things being a certain way. When the waiter came, I suggested we let him make all the food decisions. At first, there was resistance, but eventually everyone said "what the heck," and we did it. The waiter proceeded to bring out these incredible dishes that we'd never have ordered on our own.

We ended up telling each other what we really loved about each other and had one of those amazing times that we look back on and say "wow." It became a present, alive and profound meeting that we never could have planned.

Try following the motto "Show up, be present and don't be attached to the outcome." When we finally realize that we really don't have much control over how things turn out, we'll drop some of the controlling behaviors that prevent us from trying new things and living fully. When we let go of the idea that "it has to be this way," we'll experience more joy in our lives.

FOLLOW THE RULES

They say that necessity is the mother of invention, and it's amazing how we can improvise when we are working within limitations. When you've got only 10 minutes to come up with a proposal, it only takes 10 minutes. When hundreds of us were stuck at an airport for two days due to a snowstorm, many of us had a great time and made some new friends. (Some people grumbled and complained for two days.) Soon after my son was potty trained, we went for a hike and I was caught off guard by his first need to go number two in the woods. Let's just say that I walked back to the car wearing only one sock.

It can be fun and enlightening to put limitations on yourself and see what kind of creativity comes out of it. The activities in this book have a structure to follow and boundaries to stay within; you can do the same thing in your life. Give yourself limitations or conditions in which to play and have fun. I really enjoy going into a kitchen with no idea what's in the fridge or cabinets and making dinner without using a recipe. It poses a challenge to be innovative, and it forces me to improvise.

Once while I was traveling in London, a buddy and I (who both have very limited musical abilities) had a harmonica and a hat. The rule we made was that we'd play and sing on the street corner until we got one pound in change. It happened—probably more out of sympathy than anything else. Another time, while a friend and I were sitting in a movie theater waiting for the movie to start, he bet me five bucks that I couldn't get half the people in the theater to sing for 30 seconds. As people were coming in to sit down, I shook their hands and said something like "thanks for joining us today." As the people sat there watching the still-slide ads before the previews, I stood up front and announced, "Thanks for joining us here today. I'm George Jondon, the manager, and I want to take this opportunity to let you know how pleased we are that you chose our theater. We realize you have a choice..." I went on to tell them how we were testing a new procedure because we'd found that connecting with others at the theater creates a more beneficial movie experience. "We make that connection by singing a couple of songs." Then we went into "Sunshine on my shoulder..." Soon my friend paid me the five bucks. So establish some parameters, and then let it rip.

NO SIDE TALKING

This rule is really important for increasing the spontaneity and joy in your life. What I mean is that when you're creating new songs, dancing with abandon or making stuff up, don't evaluate, critique or compare—in other words, turn off your inner critic. That goes for anyone you're with, as well. We have a tendency to talk about our experience while we are experiencing it, and that just doesn't work when you're trying to be spontaneous. When kids and adults are free to create without side comments, judgments, or opinions, they feel safe and free to express themselves. Isn't it great when everyone is dancing at a wedding; it's like we're all in it together.

It also helps if the people who you are with go along with what you are doing. Once when I was golfing with my buddy John (who can keep a straight face better than anyone) we arrived at the first tee to meet the two-some we were assigned a tee time with. After the "nice to meet you, nice day" stuff, we decided I'd tee off first. As I reached for my driver, I noticed my son's driver, which is half the size of a regular golf club. I pulled it up a little, made eye contact with John, and he gave me a nod. I knew he'd support me, so I took out the club, and warmed up a bit.

As I was setting up my ball, one of the fellows we'd just met said, "Hey that must be your kid's club." I turned to him and said with a straight face, "No, actually it's the new Dunlop Minimizer." He must have thought I was joking until he turned to John who looked at him as if to say, "You mean you've never seen it before? Where the heck have you been?" It was John's playing along with it that made the joke work. I ended up hitting the ball straight down the fairway. It wasn't a long shot, but it was straight. I turned to the guy and said, "You should have seen my slice before I bought this puppy." At the next hole he asked if he could try the club, so I told him we were just kidding. When you are being spontaneous and improvising in life, it's crucial to avoid analysis or discussion.

WAYS TO IMPROVISE ON YOUR OWN

So how can you improvise on your own and become more spontaneous? Here's a short list of suggestions that should give you some ideas and help you expand your comfort zone. It is merely a starting point to get you thinking about the endless possibilities throughout your daily life.

❑ Next time you're at the mall, have a three-minute conversation with a mannequin. Really get into it, and have a friend watch the looks on people's faces from afar.

❑ Roll down your car window and sing.

❑ Give the folks at a drive-through window a round of applause and tell them you appreciate all the great work they do.

❑ Walk into a coffee shop and exclaim loudly, "My name is Chuck. Who wants to chat?"

❑ While grocery shopping, ask to say a few words over the sound system. My experience has been that one out of five times they'll say yes.

❑ Spend an hour walking randomly with nowhere to go. Just see what happens. Nowhere to go. Nothing to buy.

❑ For five minutes, give every person you pass on the street your biggest and warmest smile.

❑ Dance anywhere there is a song you like (coffee shop, grocery store, etc.).

❑ Go to a playground and play like a kid.

❑ Say "yes" when you would normally say "no."

❑ When you become self-conscious ask yourself, "Who will care 100 years from now (or even 100 days)?"

❑ Hang out with fun people.

❑ Watch a dog. Watch a squirrel. Watch a cat. Watch an ant hill.

❏ With a buddy, get the people on a plane to sing Row, Row, Row Your Boat as a round (this can work on United, not just Southwest).

❏ Buy a plastic booger and put it in your nose for a while anywhere you'd rather not (on a date, at the mall, etc.).

❏ When there's a lull at a ball game and the crowd noise is low, stand up and yell random statements with the conviction of the proudest fan. "That's what I call putting the phone on hold", "Oh yea, where's the extra cheese on that one!", "Hey ref, I got three checks to cash, and I'll be doing it tomorrow!" The more random, the better.

❏ As you're coming off a plane, and you see a group of people with banners saying "Welcome Home Mary," run up to them and hug as many as you can before Mary shows up.

❏ Buy popcorn for the person standing behind you at the movies.

❏ Put limitations on yourself. Go out for an evening without spending any money (go to the library, eat free samples at different grocery stores, hitch a ride), or only spend $5.00 (go to the dollar theater with homemade popcorn, etc.).

❏ Compliment every person you encounter today.

❏ Grab twenty one-dollar bills, make a cardboard sign that says "I've got a dollar for you if you need it," and stand on the street corner with it. See how many people roll down their windows to accept the money.

❏ Try to meet five new people today.

❏ Go to yard sales and buy something that will encourage creativity and doing something new. Then actually do something creative and new.

❏ Establish a once-a-week try-something-new evening. Things to consider: classes, museums, new church, rock gym, pottery, invent something, rec center, yoga class, play with little kids, hang out with high school kids, volunteer at the nursing home, shop at a thrift store, go to a coffee shop and play a board game, rent a horse, dog sit....

❏ Spend one night brainstorming 100 things to do with your family other than watching TV. Narrow down the list to 52 and do one per week for a year.

❏ As adults we're usually either talking about what we're going to do, or what we've done. If you notice this happening, do something. Get in the practice of being totally present to what you're doing.

ONE-HOUR SESSION

❏ **Clarify the Top Five Rules of Improv:** No Side Talking, Follow the Directions, 100% Commitment, Accept, and Don't Try to Be Funny (can be read from Appendix B)

❏ **Warm-up Activities** (page 47):

❏ **Whole Group Exercise** (Chapter 7):

❏ **Divide into Partners** (page 50):

❏ **Get-to-Know-You Exercise** (Chapter 8):

❏ **Partner Exercise** (Chapter 9):

❏ **Processing Questions** (Appendix D):

❏ **Divide into Small Groups** (page 50):

❏ **Small Group Exercise** (Chapter 10):

❏ **Processing Questions** (Appendix D):

❏ **Suggestion Question(s)** (Appendix C):

❏ **Game** (Chapter 12):

❏ **Closure Activity** (Chapter 13):

TOP FIVE RULES OF IMPROV

Rule #1 - No Side Talking: Refrain from making side comments to each other, both while doing the activity and while processing the activity. Share any insights or challenges with the whole group at the appropriate time. Everyone involved will feel safer if they know there will be no side talking or gossiping.

Rule #2 - Follow the Directions: There are specific formats or rules for every exercise and game that the players *must* follow. For example: If the description of the exercise says that each player can only speak one word at a time, only speak one word at a time, not two, not three.

Rule #3 - Commit 100%: Committing yourself 100% to the activities is the most important thing you can do to make them fun and meaningful. All people involved should give 100% to every activity or the activity will be difficult. A full 100% commitment is much easier than 90%, 70%, or even 50%. It is similar to hang gliding. You either do it or don't.

Rule #4 - Accept: Accept what the other players say and do. If another player hands you something and says, "Congratulations Johnny! You got an A on your spelling test," you immediately become a student receiving your spelling test, and you could reply with "Thanks Mrs. Barney. I even spelled schedule right."

Rule #5 - Don't Try to Be Funny: Many times people will introduce contrived material into the activities to try to be funny, smart or witty. This takes away from the possibilities of the activity and detracts from everyone's learning experience. All the activities in this book can be a lot of fun—and often end up being very funny—just by having fun versus trying to be funny.

REQUESTS AND QUESTIONS TO SOLICIT SUGGESTIONS

❏ What is your favorite thing to do on the weekend?

❏ Tell me something you hate to do around the house.

❏ Name an outdoor activity.

❏ Give me a generic location.

❏ Name a place where you would never _____ .

❏ Give me two contrasting occupations.

❏ Name a country (or a state in the US).

❏ What is a goal someone wants to achieve?

❏ Give me a word beginning with the letter C (or any letter).

❏ Name two words that don't go together.

❏ Where's a place you love to go?

❏ What's something you'd find in a junk drawer?

❏ Tell me an achievement you're proud of.

❏ Give me a major in college.

❏ Tell me a place you would never hide.

❏ What is something you would love to do?

❏ Give me a three-letter word (or four- or five-letter).

❏ Make up a title of a story that hasn't been written.

❏ Tell me an occupation that is hazardous.

❏ Give me an emotion or state of mind.

PROCESSING AND DISCUSSION QUESTIONS

Level-one questions (describe what happened)

- ❐ What are some observations about this exercise?
- ❐ What was easy (or difficult) about this exercise?
- ❐ What did you see or hear?
- ❐ What did you notice about yourself? About your partner?
- ❐ Use one word to describe what happened?

Level-two questions (share some feelings)

- ❐ How did you feel doing the exercise?
- ❐ Did you trust yourself?
- ❐ Did you trust the others in your group? Why? Why not?
- ❐ How did it feel to _____ ?
- ❐ What did others do that made you feel supported?
- ❐ What did you do to support others?
- ❐ Did you feel uncomfortable? Why? Is this familiar?

Level-three questions (make sense of what happened)

- ❐ What did you learn from this exercise?
- ❐ How does this exercise relate to _____?
  (teamwork, focus, work, etc.)
- ❐ What did you learn about communicating?
- ❐ When is it important to communicate with words?
- ❐ When are non-verbal forms of communication
  more important?
- ❐ What is trust and how do we learn to trust others?
- ❐ What was the point of this exercise?

Level-four questions (apply it to life)

- ❐ How does what you learned apply to your life?
- ❐ How is this exercise helpful for us?
- ❐ What piece of new learning can you apply to your life?
- ❐ What will you start, stop, or continue doing in your life?

Column key (game — page number):

PARTNERS: Basic Mirror (79), A to Z (78), I Love You So... (77), Ground Control (76), Trust Walk (75), Endowments Practice (74), Pass The Object (73), Non-Verbal Essence (72)

GETTING TO KNOW: Proud To Say (71), Weather Report (71), Name Game (70), Pride And Dream (70), Make It Up (69)

WHOLE GROUP: On The Spot Cheer (68), Three's A Crowd (67), Thumb Dance (66), Everybody Go... (64), Color Vision (63), Group Beat (62), Visionary (62), Standing O' (60), Criss, Cross, Clap (59), Mega Mirror (58), Way To Go (57), Another O.K. (57), O.K. (56), Clap Happy (55)

Page Number	79	78	77	76	75	74	73	72	71	71	70	70	69	68	67	66	64	63	62	62	60	59	58	57	57	56	55
DIFFICULTY	E	E	E	E	E	E	E	H	M	M	E	E	E	M	M	M	M	E	E	E	E	E	E	E	E	E	E
Acceptance	×			×	×		×			×		×		×			×					×				×	×
Attention to detail	×	×	×				×			×					×	×	×			×		×	×	×		×	
Awareness of others				×			×		×		×		×			×	×	×		×	×	×		×		×	
Conflict resolution skills						×									×												
Creativity				×		×			×				×					×							×		
Dealing with change				×		×	×										×		×								
Focus	×													×				×				×		×			×
Idea generation										×			×				×				×						
Leadership									×					×	×								×	×			
Learning about others							×				×		×														
Letting go of control					×			×								×	×				×			×			
Listening	×			×			×				×		×					×	×			×	×				×
Movement	×			×	×		×			×				×	×	×	×			×	×	×	×			×	
Non-verbal communication	×			×	×		×	×					×		×								×			×	
Not just one right answer			×						×					×		×											
Overcoming fear					×	×		×					×			×					×						
Playfulness	×			×	×			×						×	×		×			×	×			×			
Story telling						×																	×				
Supporting others	×			×	×		×						×										×				
Teamwork	×			×	×		×	×	×				×	×								×		×			×
Word choice		×	×	×		×			×																		
Verbal communication				×		×			×				×														

PARTNERS	Two Sided	Forbidden Letter	Changes	Sentence Story	Embellishment	Dis-Emblisshment	Emotional Roller Coaster	Last Letter First Letter	Scriptorama	What Are You Doing?	Switching Mirror	Yes, And...No, But...	Rhyme Lines	First And Last	Gibberish Lessons	Language Barrier	Up And Down	Countdown	Fixed Word	Sliding Mirror	Funky Mirror	Gibberish Switch	Only Questions	Talking Mirror	Sing It!	Back Talk	Five Letter Word	Emotional Seesaw	Mid-Word Story
Page Number	80	81	82	83	84	85	86	88	88	90	91	92	93	94	95	96	97	98	99	100	101	102	103	104	105	106	107	108	109
DIFFICULTY	E	M	M	M	M	M	M	M	M	M	M	M	M	M	M	M	H	H	H	H	H	H	H	H	H	H	H	H	H
Acceptance	×										×			×		×	×			×	×	×		×			×		×
Attention to detail		×	×		×											×			×	×	×		×	×		×			
Awareness of others			×							×	×			×					×	×	×		×	×				×	
Conflict resolution skills				×			×											×											
Creativity				×						×		×		×		×						×			×	×			
Dealing with change			×	×										×			×			×				×			×	×	
Focus	×						×			×	×	×	×			×	×			×	×			×			×		
Idea generation									×	×	×					×				×	×				×				
Leadership														×	×						×								
Learning about others									×																				
Letting go of control	×													×		×	×	×		×		×		×		×			×
Listening	×			×		×		×				×		×	×	×			×	×				×		×	×		×
Movement																						×		×					
Non-verbal communication	×						×		×		×	×	×	×			×		×	×		×				×		×	×
Not just one right answer	×				×				×						×	×		×			×						×		×
Overcoming fear										×															×	×			
Playfulness										×															×				
Story telling	×			×								×												×			×		
Supporting others																					×			×				×	
Teamwork					×									×										×					
Word choice	×	×															×		×	×	×		×			×	×		×
Verbal communication	×	×		×		×		×	×				×					×	×	×	×					×	×		×

216

Game (SMALL GROUP)	Page Number	DIFFICULTY	Acceptance	Attention to detail	Awareness of others	Conflict resolution skills	Creativity	Dealing with change	Focus	Idea generation	Leadership	Learning about others	Letting go of control	Listening	Movement	Non-verbal communication	Not just one right answer	Overcoming fear	Playfulness	Story telling	Supporting others	Teamwork	Word choice	Verbal communication
Stereotypes	138	M	X				X									X						X		
Living Machines	137	M	X	X			X									X					X	X		
I Didn't Go To The Store	136	M	X											X			X							
Last Line/First Line	135	M	X	X			X									X			X				X	X
Hitchhiker	134	M	X		X		X	X				X				X				X		X		
Group Effort	133	M	X		X		X	X		X					X	X					X	X		
Add A Part	133	M	X	X			X			X						X			X		X	X		
Grab Bag	132	M	X	X			X				X					X			X	X		X		
Exaggerate, Whine...	131	M	X				X			X			X			X					X			
Mime A Room	130	M	X		X				X						X	X					X			
Slow Mo Tag	129	E	X		X		X								X	X	X				X			
Walk And Roll	128	E	X				X			X		X	X		X						X	X		
Freeze Easy	127	E	X	X			X			X	X				X	X	X				X	X		
That's A Great Ideal	126	E		X			X			X			X		X	X					X	X		X
Rhythm Circle	125	E		X											X	X					X	X		X
Walka Beek	124	E				X			X				X		X				X		X	X		X
Playground	124	E				X																	X	
Emotional Line	123	E	X				X		X				X		X				X			X		
Thanks For The...	122	E	X	X	X					X			X											
Circular Mirror	121	E	X	X	X		X			X	X		X		X	X					X	X		
Pass The Movement	119	E	X	X						X	X		X		X	X								
Pass The Mask	118	E	X	X		X			X						X	X					X	X		
Pass The Clap	117	E	X			X			X						X	X					X	X		
Pass The Energy	116	E	X					X		X					X	X					X	X		
Conversation Chaos	115	E			X		X		X		X			X	X	X		X			X	X	X	X
Clear Catch	114	E	X		X		X			X			X		X	X		X			X	X		
All Talk	113	E							X					X		X							X	X
Shape Up	112	E	X	X	X		X	X			X		X		X	X					X	X		
Air Jump	112	E			X	X																	X	X
Oh No	111	E			X													X						

217

Legend of games (columns), in order, with page number and difficulty (E = Easy, M = Medium, H = Hard):

#	Game	Page	Difficulty
1	Inventory Story	138	M
2	Tug Of Air	139	M
3	To Move Or Not To Move	140	M
4	Two On One	141	M
5	Rap Circle	141	M
6	What Is It?	142	M
7	Limited Lines	143	H
8	Freeze Me Or Please Me	144	H
9	Freeze - Double Blind	145	H
10	Introduce The Speaker	146	H
11	Introduce The Introducer	147	H
12	Two Line Scene	148	H
13	Justification Line	149	H
14	Group Poetry	150	H
15	Back to the Basics	160	E
16	Arms Expert	160	E
17	The Professor	162	E
18	Two For One	163	E
19	Foreign Movie	164	E
20	Foreign Interpreter	165	E
21	Audience Sound Effects	166	E
22	Newscast	167	E
23	Slide Show	168	E
24	Crowd Control	169	E
25	Your Day Your Way	169	E
26	Conducted Story	170	M
27	No Laughs	171	M
28	End	171	M
29	Dubbing	172	M

Skills matrix (SMALL GROUP games = #1–14; GAMES / Back to the Basics = #15–29). Column numbers match the legend above.

Skill	1	2	3	4	5	6	7	8	9	10	11	12	13	14	15	16	17	18	19	20	21	22	23	24	25	26	27	28	29
Acceptance	×	×																											
Attention to detail		×	×					×	×	×	×	×	×	×			×	×		×							×		×
Awareness of others					×				×	×	×						×		×		×	×	×						×
Conflict resolution skills			×		×		×						×															×	
Creativity	×					×		×		×			×		×								×		×				
Dealing with change	×						×	×		×										×				×					
Focus	×			×	×	×		×		×		×			×		×				×			×		×		×	×
Idea generation													×				×							×		×	×		×
Leadership		×			×		×																×	×					
Learning about others																		×							×				
Letting go of control	×		×			×	×					×		×		×		×		×		×			×	×			
Listening	×	×			×	×	×					×		×		×				×		×				×		×	×
Movement	×	×	×					×					×		×	×	×				×		×	×		×	×		×
Non-verbal communication	×	×													×	×		×		×			×	×			×		
Not just one right answer													×						×			×							
Overcoming fear															×	×	×	×		×	×	×	×						
Playfulness					×												×						×						
Story telling	×										×			×		×					×			×	×	×		×	
Supporting others		×		×		×			×					×		×	×			×				×			×		×
Teamwork		×	×	×											×	×	×	×		×							×	×	×
Word choice		×	×			×					×											×						×	×
Verbal communication				×	×						×			×		×		×			×				×				

GAMES	Crossroads	Spelling Machine	Old Time Radio	Emotional Party	Entrances and Exits	Film Director	Write On	Replay	Slow Motion	Endowments Exchange	Movie Styles	Mood Swings	Forward/Reverse	Emotional Boundaries	The Thing He Said...	Scene in Verse	Hesitation	Should Have Said	Shakespeare	Sing a Song	Mannequin	Opera	Foreign Opera	Sit, Stand, Kneel	Script Scene	Broadway Musical	Radio Station Dial	Activate	Poetry	Poetry Group
Page Number	173	174	175	175	176	176	177	178	178	179	180	181	182	183	184	185	186	187	188	188	189	190	190	191	192	192	193	194	196	196
DIFFICULTY	M	M	M	M	M	M	M	M	M	M	H	H	H	H	H	H	H	H	H	H	H	H	H	H	H	H	H	H	H	H
Acceptance	×	×																												
Attention to detail						×	×			×			×	×	×		×	×			×				×					
Awareness of others			×	×	×					×				×	×			×		×		×	×				×	×		
Conflict resolution skills						×		×				×	×	×	×						×						×			
Creativity		×	×	×			×			×									×											×
Dealing with change	×			×		×								×	×		×	×	×	×	×		×	×	×	×				×
Focus								×		×	×		×						×											
Idea generation				×			×			×		×			×	×	×	×	×			×			×		×		×	×
Leadership				×		×									×	×			×			×	×					×	×	×
Learning about others																				×										
Letting go of control					×						×	×		×		×		×	×	×		×	×							
Listening					×	×	×							×		×	×		×	×	×	×	×							
Movement									×										×		×									
Non-verbal communication									×	×									×	×	×	×						×		
Not just one right answer	×	×		×					×		×	×			×	×	×	×			×			×			×	×		
Overcoming fear		×																				×	×		×					
Playfulness	×	×					×							×								×	×		×	×				
Story telling		×	×			×	×															×	×		×	×				
Supporting others	×	×					×					×													×	×				
Teamwork	×	×		×			×		×				×					×				×	×		×	×			×	×
Word choice	×	×			×		×							×		×	×							×		×			×	×
Verbal communication	×	×					×							×	×	×	×			×									×	×

219

Notes

Notes

ABOUT POSITIVELY HUMOR

A NATIONALLY KNOWN speaker and consultant, Craig is unlike any one else you've heard—never scripted, yet always insightful. He's been called a hybrid of Robin Williams and Wayne Dyer. The dozens of national associations Craig has keynoted for include the National Teacher Educators Association, the National Boys and Girls Clubs of America, and the National Principals Association. He has also worked extensively with numerous corporations including Microsoft, Disney, and Wells Fargo.

Craig has taught the concepts of this book through individually tailored programs for businesses, educators, health-care professionals, students, government employees and nonprofit groups. He challenges group members to get out of their own way to experience more laughter, creativity, confidence, truth and joy in their lives. Participants learn to take themselves lightly and to see their inherent greatness, both individually and organizationally.

Craig offers inspirational keynotes, workshops, weekend seminars and executive coaching. His many programs include:

Learning and Laughter – Making the Connection

Life is Improvisation – Jump … Design Your Wings as You Go

Authentic Leadership – The Truest Part of Leadership Is Not What You Think

Humor, Health and Healing – A Program for People Going Through Major Transitions

This Is It – Grasping the Power of NOW

For more information on Craig's programs or his other books, CDs and videos, check out his website at www.positivelyhumor.com or call 303-830-7996.

ABOUT THE AUTHOR

AFTER GRADUATING FROM Colorado State University with a degree in finance, Craig went on to manage a popular chain restaurant. The tragic death of his sister caused him to question the value of a life in business, so after traveling for a while, he went back to school and became a high school teacher in an inner-city school. Accepting an invitation to join a professional improv troupe on the weekends led to him incorporating the principles of improvisation in his classroom. He was inspired by the way improvisation helped the high-risk kids he taught to open up and develop more positive self esteem, so he decided to take these ideas to the masses.

Craig established his company Positively Humor in 1993 and has since spoken to hundreds of thousands of people about how to lighten up and experience more freedom and joy by using the principles of improvisation in their daily lives. He's shared the platform with Tom Peters and Al Gore, and he delivered his Humor and Healing program to the student body of Columbine High School soon after its tragedy. Craig's ideas have been published in numerous articles and he's co-authored two other books, Humor Me and Humor Us.

Denver, Colorado is home to Craig and his incredible son Charles, also know as Cha Cha, or Chuka Mooka.

ORDERING INFORMATION

💻 **On-line orders:** PositivelyHumor.com

☎ **Telephone orders:** 1(303) 830-7996. Have your VISA or MasterCard ready.

🖨 **Fax orders:** Photo copy back side of this page and fax to: 1(303) 830-0194

✉ **Postal orders** Photocopy back side of this page and mail to:

POSITIVELY HUMOR

634 Marion Street, Suite 102

Denver, CO 80218

Please send me _____ copies of

IMPROV 101: EXERCISES TO UNLEASH YOUR CREATIVE SPIRIT

at $19.95 for each copy.

Name: _____

Address: _____

City: _____ **State:** _____

Zip: _____

Telephone:

(_____) _____

Sales tax: Please add 4.1% for books shipped to Colorado addresses.

Shipping: Add $3.00 for the first book and $1.00 for each additional book.

Payment:

    Check for _____

    Credit card: VISA or MasterCard Card number:

    _____

    Name on card: _____

    Exp. Date: _____ /_____

    Code _____ (last 3 digits on back of card)

Signature: _____

PHOTOCOPY THIS PAGE TO ORDER BY MAIL OR FAX